Grand master baths

Grand master baths

Janice Costa

CREATIVE HOMEOWNER®, Upper Saddle River, New Jersey

GRAND MASTER BATHS

SENIOR EDITOR	Kathie Robitz
EDITOR	Lisa Kahn
SENIOR GRAPHIC DESIGN COORDINATOR	Glee Barre
PHOTO COORDINATOR	Robyn Poplasky
JUNIOR EDITOR	Jennifer Calvert
DIGITAL IMAGING SPECIALIST	Frank Dyer
INDEXER	Schroeder Indexing Services
COVER DESIGN	Glee Barre
FRONT COVER PHOTOGRAPHY	(center) Omega Cabinetry; (top right) Kohler Company; (bottom right) Sawhill Custom Kitchens & Design, Inc.
BACK COVER PHOTOGRAPHY	(top left) St. Charles Cabinetry; (bottom left) Omega Cabinetry; (bottom center) Carol Kurth, AIA, The Office of Carol J.W. Kurth, AIA Architect, pc; photography by Peter Krupenye

CREATIVE HOMEOWNER

VICE PRESIDENT AND PUBLISHER	Timothy O. Bakke
PRODUCTION DIRECTOR	Kimberly H. Vivas
ART DIRECTOR	David Geer
MANAGING EDITOR	Fran J. Donegan

Current Printing (last digit)
10 9 8 7 6 5 4 3 2 1

Grand Master Baths, First Edition
Library of Congress Control Number: 2007933865
ISBN-10: 1-58011-388-5
ISBN-13: 978-1-58011-388-5
CREATIVE HOMEOWNER®
A Division of Federal Marketing Corp.
24 Park Way
Upper Saddle River, NJ 07458
www.creativehomeowner.com

dedication

This one's for Gail Plotnick, who has been reading my words since the sixth grade, and whose continued faith, support, and friendship have been instrumental in my continuing to write them. GE, your willingness to believe in me no matter what has not only made me a better writer, it's made me a better person, and I am forever grateful to have you in my life. Yens and Yails forever!

acknowledgments

Writing a book is never a solitary endeavor (though it may seem like one at 3 a.m. when you're staring, bleary-eyed, at a pile of dog-stomped page proofs, doing that one last read-through). There are so many people who help take a book from conception to creation, and I have been blessed with many wonderful colleagues, supporters, and friends who have been instrumental in bringing this book to life. I would especially like to thank:

My wonderful KBDN family, including my publisher Eliot Sefrin, who has always been an inspiration to me; my terrific editorial team: Anita Shaw, John Filippelli, Barbara Capella Loehr, and Andrea Girolamo, who have been ever supportive; my wonderfully helpful artists, Ingrid Volkerts and Laura Froehlich, without whom I would still be trying to turn jpegs into tiff files; my production manager Noble Laird, who has many hidden art and computer talents and is always generous about sharing them; and the best sales team ever: Chris Kirkby, Joanne Naylor, Kim Carroll, Rick Dahl, Nancy Campoli, and Tim Steingraber.

The wonderful design professionals who were so generous about sharing their knowledge, experience, advice, and projects for this book, especially Chris Abbate; Ellen Cheever, CMKBD, ASID; Tom Cohn; Karen Dry; Cheryl Hamilton-Gray, CKD; Julie Howes; Karla Krengel; Carol J. Weissman Kurth, AIA, Allied Member ASID; Steve Nicholls; Mollyanne Sherman, CKD, CBD, CID; Julie Stoner, ASID, CKD; Gaye Weatherly; and Gary White, CMKBD, CID.

The people who keep me sane (or some approximation thereof) during even the craziest deadline crunches: Mom and Dad, Kathleen and Philip Delakas, Barbara and Charles Garnar, Bob Dealy, Carol Lamb, Jeannine Gomiela, the BFDT crew, and of course, Jessie, Cody and Caspar.

And last but not least, my wonderful agent, Stephany Evans of FinePrint Literary Management, and all the terrific people at Creative Homeowner, including my editor Lisa Kahn, senior designer Glee Barre, photo coordinator Robyn Poplasky (who patiently dealt with my five million questions about sending photos, and never once picked up the phone and said "Oh, it's her again!"— at least not out loud!), and senior editor Kathie Robitz, who believed in this project from the beginning.

My heartfelt thanks go out to all of you!

Contents

Introduction

BELOW Mixing tile designs in a single color creates a feeling of subtle elegance in this bath.

OPPOSITE Skylights are a wonderful way to bring natural light into the room.

It's the most private space in your home, a personal sanctuary where you can escape the stresses of day-to-day life and rejuvenate your body, mind, and spirit. A truly grand master bath can transform your life by ensuring that you have a serene yet functional spot to start and end each day. No wonder the master bathroom is one of the most remodeled rooms in the house.

While other spaces may be designed for their "show-off" potential, the master bath is about personal luxury and private comfort. It's a place for self-indulgence, quiet reflection, and glorious solitude.

Grand Master Baths was written to help you create your dream space—one that will pamper, soothe, invigorate, and inspire you. What is your master bath fantasy? For instance, can you imagine soaking in an aromatherapy bath near a fireplace, with scented candles burning and a glass of chilled wine resting on the tub deck? Or sharing a two-person supershower with your significant other with music wafting from recessed speakers and towels warming on a heated rack? Perhaps you envision a relaxing and therapeutic whirlpool bath with built-in chromatherapy lights that uplift your spirits and prepare you for the busy day ahead?

Then again, your idea of paradise might be nothing more than 30 minutes of quiet time without a ringing phone, squabbling kids, or a large dog waiting to be walked. For a busy parent, there are built-in coffeemakers and refrigerator drawers, showers that automatically heat to your exact tem-

perature preference, and wall tiles that create a retreat so soundproof that you won't be disturbed by the stresses of the day ahead until you've had your first cup of caffeine and a hot shower.

Indeed, the array of luxury bath products on the market today makes it easier than ever to create a distinctive haven that perfectly suits your lifestyle, your budget, and your preferences. Don't have a lot of square footage? No worries! There are a host of space-saving tricks that can transform even the tiniest bathroom into an exclusively-for-you retreat. However, if space is abundant, why not plan a whole master suite, including a walk-in closet, separate dressing room, private

sitting room, mini-kitchen, and even a home gym? Do your tastes run to Tahitian-style beach houses? A villa in Tuscany? A glamorous boudoir suitable for a Hollywood movie star? Do you secretly hanker for a quaint Victorian sitting room or a contemporary space with cutting-edge technology? Or would you simply like a bathroom that's easy to clean, with plenty of storage to hide all your clutter? Whether your passion runs to colored beach glass or rich Italian tile, a remote-control programmable shower, or countertops with built-in antibacterial properties, there are products to help you realize your vision.

Grand Master Baths offers ideas and guidance for creating the master bathroom of your dreams by taking you on an exploration of the many options currently available. The journey begins with information that will help you to choose your design style; it continues with descriptions of the many new materials for vanities, floors, walls, faucets, tubs, and other products now on the market. You'll learn how to plan a lighting scheme, incorporate safety features, and select from a wealth of high-tech conveniences and luxurious finishing touches for your bath.

You'll also draw inspiration from hundreds of photos showcasing a wide array of bath designs, from Old World splendor to Modern chic. From these, you will begin to develop a clear view of the master bathroom that ideally suits your needs.

OPPOSITE Use towels to pick up your bath's accent color without overpowering the space.

BELOW This mirror cleverly contains a TV for catching your favorite morning show while you shave or apply makeup.

your private

sanctuary

1

E-mails. Voice mails. Blackberries. Text messages. Today, you have the capability to reach people at any moment. Unfortunately, this miracle of modern communication means that everyone can reach you just as easily. The stress that this adds to daily life seems like a steep price to pay for today's technological advancements.

*I*s it any surprise, then, that some days all you want to do is escape from the constant jangling of your cell phone to a place where no one can bother you?

Enter the master bathroom, the one room in the house where seclusion still reigns supreme. Even in today's high-style homes—increasingly designed for public display and admiration—the master bath is for your eyes only.

In the not-too-distant past, bathrooms were strictly utilitarian. Today, many homeowners are building master baths with all the accoutrements of a luxurious hotel or spa. This upscale trend is far more than an extravagant indulgence; it's a wise investment in one's health, happiness, and well-being. A beautiful master bathroom is a sanctuary where you can fortify your mind and body in order to meet the rigorous demands of contemporary life.

DEFINING YOUR ESCAPE PLAN

The first step in creating the grand master bath of your dreams is to compile a wish list. What does your fantasy bathroom look like? Do you imagine a romantic setting, complete with soaking tub, scented candles, and soft mood lighting? Or would you prefer a peaceful place to practice your yoga poses before jumping into a bracing steam shower? Perhaps your idea of sybaritic perfection is to sip your first cup of coffee, watch the

TOP LEFT Nothing soothes the soul like Mother Nature. For maximum comfort, think light and bright, and let simple elements like water and space define your bath's ambience.

BOTTOM LEFT Positioning a tub to take advantage of natural light makes a daily bath a delightful treat.

OPPOSITE Elegant light fixtures highlight this bath's striking mirror, making it a visual focal point, while draped window treatments "frame" the spectacular tub.

the morning news, and check the day's stock prices, all from the comfort of a bubbling spa tub.

Think about a bathroom you enjoyed while vacationing at a resort or spa. What impressed you most? Was it the heated floors? The towel warmers? The two-person shower with personalized water-temperature controls? The generous vanity and storage space? Or was it the elegant little extras, such as a built-in magnifying mirror, his and her sinks, silent exhaust fan, or crystal-encrusted faucets?

Don't rule out anything that might seem unattainable; there's technology out there that will astound you, and much of it is less expensive than you might think. Even if an option you like is out of your price range, don't abandon your dream: a good designer who understands what you'd like to accom-

ABOVE For a simple, elegant look with masculine appeal, black is always in style.

RIGHT Abundant natural light and a quiet sitting area make this bath a perfect place to retreat from the stresses of day-to-day living.

plish may help you come up with an affordable alternative that can capture the essence of your vision.

Next, do some research. Page through interior design books and magazines; visit model homes and show houses in your area; check out design Web sites; and peruse a few bath and decorative plumbing and hardware showrooms. Attending open houses in upscale neighborhoods will also help you build

design for life

When planning your dream bath, it's very easy to be seduced by the endless array of choices. How can you not be enticed by a jetted tub that incorporates mood lighting, surround-sound, and Internet access?

It's important to remember that your design plan should reflect your lifestyle. Sure, that deep soaking tub is gorgeous, but if you haven't found time for a long soak since 1993, maybe you'd be happier if you chose a spacious shower with all the upgrades.

Similarly, if your morning routine involves six different hair products and enough makeup to stock a department store, stark minimalism is probably not the style for you. Instead, think about incorporating an expansive grooming station with plenty of organized storage areas.

Do you head to your bathroom to relax, rejuvenate, and escape from the rest of the world? If so, why not maximize your precious "me" time with piped-in audio, a sitting area, a deep soaking tub, or even a fireplace? Conversely, if your morning routine is all about speed, choose a shower with temperature presets, so you needn't waste time fiddling to get the water just right.

Consider maintenance issues, too, especially if your bath will have multiple users. High-gloss surfaces, leather tiles, or intricately styled faucets with lots of tiny crevices all make gorgeous design statements, but they require extra upkeep to keep them looking great.

Remember, your master bath should be a place that helps you unwind; not one that adds more stress to your life; so be sure that your design incorporates all the elements you require for comfort and relaxation.

your idea file. Once you have a better sense of what you like, make a list of the amenities you want most in order of their priority. Next, ask yourself what you dislike about your current bathroom. Is the space cramped or poorly configured? Does it suffer from a lack of storage, light, or counter space? If multiple users share your bath, can two people get ready simultaneously, or do you get in each other's way?

This is also a good time to address existing safety problems. For example, does your bathroom have a floor that is slippery when wet, medicine cabinets that can be opened by small children, or a faucet that goes from cold to scalding hot for no apparent reason? Add these issues to your list. And

by the way...

While it's wonderful to have a palatial bathroom, never let a lack of space prevent you from having the grand master bath of your dreams. Clever design features come in all shapes and sizes, and many of the best luxury amenities take up no space at all!

TOP Blending materials such as glass and metal lends dimension to your bath design. Here, the wall-mounted faucet adds a sophisticated touch.

LEFT This bath provides a streamlined look while maintaining separate his and hers spaces to simplify the morning routine.

OPPOSITE If simplicity is your goal, consider built-in storage in the tub surround, an ingenious way to preserve the clean lines of the space.

remember to include a grab bar for the shower. Don't worry—you won't ruin your beautiful plan. The newest grab bars are a testament to high style, and they will protect you and your family from dangerous falls. In fact, many top designers insist on including them in every new bath project.

Finally, decide on the overall feeling you want your new bath to conjure. Because your ideal retreat should provide both emotional and physical comfort, consider whether you want your bath to be soft and soothing, subtly elegant, or lively and invigorating. As later chapters discuss how to combine elements such as color, lighting, and materials, you will learn how to construct a space that evokes the responses you desire.

SIZE MATTERS

Once you've completed your wish list, it's time to ponder the question of square footage. Does your existing bath meet your space requirements? Is it too small or, even, too large?

Like the old adage that you can never be too thin or too rich, many people assume that you can never have a bathroom that is "too big." In truth, an overly large space may actually be quite uncomfortable. Just as a tiny room can be confining, a giant area can make you feel exposed and uneasy. What's more, bathrooms that are too large can echo unpleasantly, creating a feeling of coldness rather than warmth.

Obviously, a super-size bathroom can also be a wonderful

luxury. Given ample room, you can pick and choose from a host of delightful amenities. Abundant counter and storage space is chief among them, but how about a two-person tub or shower (or both), dual grooming stations, a private bidet, or even a mini-kitchen, exercise area, or spa? Just keep in mind that with a large floor plan, you'll need to separate your master bath into functional areas, or zones, either through fixture placement or the artful use of color and materials. By doing so, you'll maintain a sense of warmth, create a better flow, and muffle excess sound.

Of course, square footage is not the sole feature that makes a bath luxurious, nor does a shortage of space mean you can't have a stunning and stylish retreat. If space is at a premium, you still have several options.

Steal from existing space. Talk with a designer about the many clever ways you can borrow space from an extra bedroom, closet, or hallway, or even create shared closet space between rooms.

Use space–saving products and solutions. If you are limited to an existing footprint, consider such options as a corner tub, pocket doors, wall-mounted faucets, and pedestal sinks, all designed to take up minimal square footage. Replacing an existing tub with a luxurious shower is another increasingly popular solution. If you already have a second bathroom with a tub you rarely use, this may be an excellent space-saving idea that doesn't sacrifice anything you really want.

Get creative with storage. Lack of floor space doesn't mean you can't have plenty of functional storage. There are many ways to build storage space into your bath that don't waste precious square footage. These solutions are light years beyond a few shelves above the toilet or a wicker basket on the floor for storing extra towels. For example, there are new cabinet styles that come in an L-shape configuration that sits on two walls, doubling the storage capacity of a standard cabinet. Some new tubs offer built-in storage, and many showers feature recessed niches for soaps and shampoos. There are even full-length, door-hung mirrors on the market that open to reveal storage space for jewelry and medicine.

LEFT Mixing classic white with eye–catching patterned tile in soft shades of brown makes this space feel serene without sacrific–ing visual inter–est. Open storage and soft curves add to the bath's appeal.

by the way...

The essence of good design begins with the concept. The ambiance, the mood, the palette—all contribute to the success of the space. Think relaxation, luxury, and function when you plan your master bath.

LEFT Let your bath transport you to the place you love best, whether it's a simple beachside cottage or a romantic villa in Tuscany.

OPPOSITE Transitional style is both timeless and versatile, making it a perfect choice to complement almost any decor.

designer insights

HOW DO YOU TURN your boring bathroom into the master bath of your dreams? Designer Carol J. Weissman Kurth, AIA, Allied Member ASID, offers these suggestions:

◆ Luxury doesn't need to be large. Instead, it's the quality of the space that counts. Interesting ceilings, textures, and details all add to the depth and quality of the design.

◆ Build upon the theme. Layer and integrate design elements to enhance the architecture of the room and capture your unique personality.

◆ Display special collectibles. Niches for candles and towels and other creative ideas are all important facets of good bathroom design.

◆ Eliminate clutter. Cabinetry and places for toiletries ensure that everything is in its rightful place.

◆ Use a variety of lighting. From task lights for shaving to decorative lights that create magical moods, the importance of the right lighting cannot be overstated.

STYLE SENSATIONS

Not so long ago, bathroom designs fell into very specific categories. There were two major style choices—traditional and contemporary—with a specific delineation between the two that left no room for a middle ground. The prevailing rules of interior decor also dictated that your bathroom had to match the style of the rest of your home, regardless of how well this met your needs.

Thankfully, there has been a growing movement in the last few years toward "transitional" design, which incorporates the best elements of contemporary and traditional styles. Combine this with the equally hot trend of mixing and matching materials, and today's design choices have become more fluid, not only in a specific room, but also from room to room.

But why go for "matchy-matchy" when you can layer different textures and materials that add depth, dimension, and your own personal flair? Today, it's perfectly okay to mix natural stone, bronze, glass, and mahogany or to combine Italian tile with a clean-lined, wall-mounted faucet.

That's not to suggest that anything goes. Combining a hodgepodge of styles and materials without a basic understanding of design principles can result in a big mess. That's why it's a good idea to consult with a qualified design professional for guidance with your project.

ABOVE Contrasting the rich warmth of wood with the natural variations of stone adds depth and dimension to this impressive master bath.

RIGHT Why not add a bit of "retro" glamour to your private sanctuary? Here, a private grooming nook features an ornately designed mirror and glittery, metallic tiles.

OPPOSITE Water is an essential part of the mood and ambiance of your bath. Here, water acts as sculpture, contributing to the artistic sense of the space.

PICKING A PRO

You wouldn't entrust your health to a guy who sells miracle cures on late-night television. Neither would you assign your master bath project—or your money—to someone who is not a licensed, experienced professional. Hiring a designer or contractor with a good track record and strong professional partnerships helps to minimize problems and ensure that your project gets done quickly and efficiently. Interview several designers; study their portfolios; visit jobs they've completed; and discuss in detail what you have in mind, watching for cues to see whether you're both on the same wavelength. ✦

the ABCs of bath design

TRANSLATING PROFESSIONAL CERTIFICATIONS
Bath design, like any field, has its own special language. So when checking out designers, don't be surprised if the letters after their names read a bit like alphabet soup. Many designers are members of professional associations that help them to further their education and skills. Others pursue special certifications as proof of their knowledge and experience.

How does all this translate into finding the right designer for you? It pays to know what their designations mean. For instance, some associations require little more than annual dues, while others monitor their members to ensure that they maintain high-quality standards. Likewise, certification requirements can range from a specified number of classroom hours to proof of specialized knowledge in a variety of areas. These requirements will vary based on the governing body.

Here are some of the common abbreviations you'll see and what they mean. For more information about each organization, visit the following Web sites.

- ✦ **AIA:** Member of the American Institute of Architects; www.aia.org
- ✦ **ASID:** Member of the American Society of Interior Designers; www.asid.org
- ✦ **CBD:** Certified Bath Designer; www.nkba.org
- ✦ **CMKBD:** Certified Master Kitchen and Bath Designer; www.nkba.org
- ✦ **CAPS:** Certified Aging-in-Place Specialist; www.nari.org
- ✦ **CKBR:** Certified Kitchen & Bath Remodeler; www.nari.org
- ✦ **CR:** Certified Remodeler; www.nari.org
- ✦ **DPHA:** Member of the Decorative Plumbing & Hardware Association; www.dpha.net
- ✦ **GCP:** Green Certified Professional; www.nari.org
- ✦ **NARI:** Member of the National Association of the Remodeling Industry; www.nari.org
- ✦ **NKBA:** Member of the National Kitchen & Bath Association; www.nkba.org

natural

instincts

2

hether it's richly veined marble, warm mahogany, or the glow of the sun through a generous skylight, the celebration of all things "natural" is the leading trend in bathroom design right now. After all, there's no better choice for creating a restful sanctuary than to incorporate rejuve-nating elements from the great outdoors.

*T*here are good reasons why parents urge their children to "go outside and get some fresh air". Humans instinctively seek a connection with nature because its elements are necessary for our physical and emotional health.

WELCOMING IN THE OUTDOORS

Natural light is essential for producing vitamin D, boosting our immune systems, and strengthening teeth and bones. It can also increase energy levels, reduce eye strain, and act as a mood enhancer. By contrast, a lack of sunlight causes the brain to overproduce melatonin, which makes people feel listless.

Similarly, "fresh" outdoor air is up to 80 times less polluted than indoor air, say many experts. And natural materials, unlike their synthetic counterparts, are less likely to emit formaldehyde and other noxious chemicals.

So strong is the human love of living things that there is a scientific term for the phenomenon, *biophilia*, coined in 1984 by Harvard biologist Edward O. Wilson.

In simple terms, biophilic design draws on elements of the outdoors to make our indoor spaces both physically and psychologically satisfying. Unlike "green" design, which focuses on protecting natural resources, biophilic design is more concerned with the relaxing effects nature has on people.

Light, color, textures, and materials all play key roles in creating a beautiful master bath that looks as if it were designed by Mother Nature herself.

TOP A frameless shower blends seamlessly with this softly hued bath, keeping the look clean and open.

LEFT A low-key color scheme helps to create a space that soothes the body, mind, and soul.

OPPOSITE A lighter shade on the ceiling draws the eye upward, adding a sense of height to the space.

natural elements help create a beautiful master bath

organic contemporary

ABOVE Clean lines, a neutral color palette, and plenty of natural light are all hallmarks of organic contemporary style.

WHEN YOU HEAR THE WORD "ORGANIC," do you think of health-food stores, pesticide-free produce, and whole-grain, no-sugar bread and cookies?

The organic movement encompasses far more than our mealtime choices. Increasingly, it's becoming a way of life for those who want to take better care of their minds, bodies, and souls. Organic is about living healthy, and that means not only eating good food but also breathing clean air, drinking pure water, safely enjoying natural light, and avoiding negative elements such as noise, clutter, and harmful chemicals. Ultimately, an organic lifestyle means an increased awareness of our deep connection with the natural world.

It's not surprising, then, that the organic trend has come to define entire environments. This in turn has spawned a burgeoning new design arena, one that melds the clean, airy feeling of contemporary design with the warmth and richness of earth, sea, and sky.

The result is something designers call "organic contemporary," a style that espouses the clean lines and streamlined look of contemporary design—with a twist. Instead of the stark, high-gloss look so popular in European contemporary design, organic contemporary features nature-inspired materials; a soft, warm color palette; and an abundance of textures. The goal is to create a feel-good space that is both pleasurable and healthful. Although the initial appearance is one of serene simplicity, the variation of textures, tones, and natural materials adds a depth and complexity that resonates with many of today's homeowners.

The benefits of organic contemporary design are especially notable in the master bath, where a nature-inspired ambiance is not only visually appealing but also soothing to the psyche.

For those who want a bathroom that's trendy yet timeless, calming but also bright and uplifting, organic contemporary is a great style that works well with nearly any decor. Because the look combines elements of modern and traditional styling, it has natural movement from the play of light, space, and materials.

If healthy living is a priority, a perfect starting point is the bathroom—the first room you visit in the morning and the last place you go before bedtime. And even if you still prefer your cookies with a little sugar, organic contemporary could be the perfect design style for your master bath.

NATURE'S PALETTE

Most people envision earth tones and neutrals such as brown, beige, and cream when they think of "natural" colors. But nature's palette is far more vibrant, encompassing a rainbow of hues that reflects the earth, sun, sea, and sky.

For example, you can choose from a profusion of watercolor blues in everything from tiles, to toilets, to glass-topped, backlit vanities. In fact, according to the Color Marketing Group, a nonprofit association of designers that pre-

dicts color trends, blue will be a popular choice for baths over many years to come.

You'll find these blues in sophisticated pairings with deep-sea green and a glimmer of violet and indigo, accented with mother-of-pearl and sand to create a warming balance. It's a color palette reminiscent of the ocean that's particularly suited for a soothing and relaxing bath experience.

If you prefer something a bit warmer, there are also lush corals, rich coppers, and grassy greens in everything from wall-

coverings to floor tiles. And if you really want to jazz things up, you might consider a splash or two of bright orange, reminiscent of a brilliant sunset.

Of course, not everyone is comfortable with such bold colors in the bath. After years of all-white tiles, tubs, and toilets, many of us still prefer neutrals that never go out of style. There's good news for those folks with resale value on their minds: today's neutrals are much more exciting, thanks to tone-on-tone patterns and plenty of textural variations.

You can also give a neutral bath a boost by combining different shades within the same color family, a visual trick that creates a feeling of contrast and movement, ties a larger space together, or makes a small space seem larger.

In baths with lower ceilings, focusing the lighter shade in the upper third of the room gives the illusion of added height. Similarly, running a darker shade around the perimeter of a too-large bath can warm up the space and make it feel cozier. And using a bold splash of color in an accent such as a handpainted wall mural, a multihued light fixture, or a stained glass window can really spice up an otherwise neutral space.

OPPOSITE A variety of surface textures creates a bath with plenty of interest and contrast.

ABOVE RIGHT Vivid blues, browns, and oranges reflect the colors of nature at its most dramatic.

RIGHT Nature–inspired colors don't have to be muted earth tones. Rich reds that mimic the colors of a stunning sunset can provide dramatic contrast to neutral floors and fixtures.

mother nature's palette encompasses

a rainbow of hues

FAR LEFT Designing the bath to incorporate greenery both indoors and out improves the air quality as well as the ambiance. The log beams and roughhewn door and window frames add a rustic appeal.

ABOVE A simple yet striking layout can help minimize clutter. Look for unusual linear treatments for walls, flooring, and vanity surfaces that complement one another.

LEFT Treasures from the ocean add a variety of natural tones and textures.

LET THERE BE LIGHT

Nothing brightens a space like plenty of natural light. Bathrooms with abundant light offer many benefits, from mood enhancement and extra safety to true color rendering when applying makeup or selecting the right tie to match a suit.

But what if your bath's location doesn't allow for windows? Skylights and sun tunnels are popular options because they flood the room with light and warmth, a real energy saver in winter. Or, you can take advantage of the light from an adjoining room, as well as create a more open layout, by opening the bath up to a master bedroom.

If windows already exist but are small or poorly located, you can position mirrors so that incoming light is reflected around the room, amplifying the effect.

You can also employ mood lighting not only to simulate morning, afternoon, and evening effects, but to ensure that makeup and clothing look their best for any environment.

Finally, numerous companies now manufacture full-spectrum lighting products that offer many of the benefits of natural light without the need to knock down walls.

by the way...

To reproduce the experience of an upscale hotel in your own bath, think under-floor heating, well-lit mirrors, and speakers for music installed directly into the walls. Even a CD player or MP3 player with speakers can play your favorite tunes while you soak blissfully in the tub.

RIGHT High ceilings can help to create a light and airy space with a spa–like feel. Here, the vaulted ceiling heightens the drama of the luxurious tub, which is a focal point for the room.

mirrors are great for

LEFT For those who love classic white but don't want a too-stark space, consider a nature-inspired accent color on one wall. Adding texture to a white floor and tub deck can also help to rejuvenate the classic white of yesteryear.

BELOW Centering the tub between several windows adds visual symmetry while bringing the bather closer to the great outdoors. Privacy blinds allow you to enjoy natural light without being visible to those outdoors.

OPPOSITE Mirrors are a great way to visually expand a space and double the impact of the existing lighting.

expanding a space and doubling the impact of existing lighting

designer insights

There's no question that Mother Nature is the ultimate design professional. Her ingenious blend of colors, textures, and other sensory delights can bring any space to life. So how do you tap into the artistry of nature to create a genuinely beautiful master bath? According to designer Ellen Cheever, CMKBD, ASID, of Wilmington, Delaware–based Ellen Cheever & Associates, the key is to maximize views to bring the outdoors in, avoid shiny surfaces and faux materials, and choose understated colors reminiscent of the earth and sea.

The following are Cheever's suggestions for creating a master bathroom retreat with plenty of natural appeal.

✦ One of the best ways to create a nature–inspired feeling is to let the outdoors in. Determine what, if any, views are accessible from the windows. If the outdoor scene is less than inspiring, consider adding a skylight, replacing a window with a French door, or even creating a faux balcony.

✦ Define which natural materials mean the most to you. Perhaps it's handmade ceramic tile, bamboo cabinets, or grass–cloth wallpaper. To maximize your bathroom's appeal, choose materials that strike a personal chord.

✦ Be cautious about using synthetic products that merely look like natural materials. A vinyl floor that resembles pebbles is less appealing than a tile floor made with real pebbles. If the real thing is too rustic or difficult to maintain, consider an accent piece in a real material to add visual impact.

✦ Keep an eye on the sheen of various bath surfaces. Most elements in nature are weathered and roughened, so if a natural look is your goal, avoid slick and shiny textures.

✦ Choose colors that reflect the mood you want to create. Imagine the ethereal blues, natural browns, beautiful greens, and silvery golds of the earth, sea, and sky–colors that are soft, soothing, and understated. For a look with more drama, consider rich oranges that reflect a vibrant sunset.

✦ Be sure your accessories sustain the back-to-nature theme. Jarring elements such as bright purple towels or obviously synthetic window treatments can dramatically diminish the effect of a nature–inspired bath. To maximize the look, keep it consistent.

MATERIAL DECISIONS

One of the biggest trends in bath design has been the return to natural materials, and the number of options available today is truly dazzling. Earthy stone, granite, slate, and travertine are extremely popular; while marble is still a top choice for those seeking a classically elegant look and feel.

When it comes to surfaces, shiny is out; honed is in. Fortunately, the roughhewn, weathered look is not only visually appealing, it's also less likely to show dirt and fingerprints. Another advantage to unpolished materials is that they are relatively slip-resistant, meaning less chance of a dangerous fall on a wet floor.

From maple and cherry to exotic wenge, zebra, and mahogany, woods lend warmth and character to bath surfaces,

and designers are choosing it in greater numbers. Bamboo, an environmentally friendly material because of its rapid regrowth, is another popular choice that is appearing in everything from vanities to flooring (even towels), the byproduct of an interior design trend toward Asian decor and quiet, Zen-like spaces. And if you're looking for a truly cutting-edge accent material, leather tiles can look fabulous around mirrors and other areas that don't get splashed.

Thanks to its beauty, versatility, and light-reflecting qualities, glass is making a big statement in the form of translucent tiles, shelves, and for the ultimate focal point, glass, backlit vanity tops in stunning colors.

In faucets and finishes, the vintage look is in. Oil-rubbed bronze, wrought iron, and weathered bronzes and coppers add

RIGHT For a smaller space, consider muted elegance rather than over-the-top drama. Here, the shower boasts a striking pattern that is eye-catching yet subtle enough not to detract from the rest of the room.

more richness and elegance to the bath than the standard, oh-so-shiny chrome.

Having trouble deciding which material works best for your bath retreat? You needn't worry because mixing and matching is all the rage. You'll find plenty of fixtures and materials on the market now that will allow you to personalize your master-bath environment without having to conform to a particular style category. Just as in nature, a well-balanced blend of colors and textures is sure to soothe and inspire you.

SENSORY INDULGENCES

One of the remarkable things about nature is that it indulges all five senses. From the fragrance of blooming spring flowers to the taste of a delicate snowflake on the tongue to the sensation of a crisp autumn breeze or the soothing sounds of a summer rain shower, Mother Nature is adept at providing a complete sensory experience each and every day.

Nature isn't something to be admired from afar; it's something to be experienced. And one of the most amazing things

about the natural world is that everyone experiences it differently. Perhaps that's why so many of us find the great outdoors to be so incredibly soothing, invigorating, and joyful.

Is it any surprise that in the most personal of rooms, elements of nature provide the perfect backdrop for re-creating all its sensory delights? From waterfall showerheads to aromatherapy tubs to swirling, bubbling air baths to cool stone vanity tops, the master bath is about touch, smell, sound, and sensation. In short, it's all about the experience.

Sure, it's important to have a space for cleansing and getting ready to face the day. But why not incorporate elements that transform the bath from just a functional space to a true sanctuary, designed to appeal to both body and soul? Whether it's finding inner peace, getting an exhilarating jump start on the day, or simply taking a few minutes to unwind, spending time in the bath can be the perfect way to commune with the outdoors, enjoying all of the sensory pleasures Mother Nature provides, without ever leaving the house! ◆

by the way...

Your master bath should be a calm, quiet retreat, but loud music or a TV can create jarring echoes when the sound bounces off tile and other hard surfaces. Make sure to include cushioning materials such as large, fluffy towels and fabric window treatments into the space. These soft touches will add that extra bit of luxury to an already spa-like experience.

OPPOSITE Natural stone offers an array of colors and patterns that add depth and dimension to this bath.

RIGHT Separate zones can make a bath more efficient, but too many walls can create a space that's more claustrophobic than cozy. Here, interesting arches open up the bath and draw the light throughout the space.

light and air are natural mood lifters

ABOVE To open up the bath, run a lighter palette seamlessly across the floor and walls; then contrast with a darker color on the vanity and around the mirror.

OPPOSITE TOP LEFT A separate grooming station set apart from the vanity allows one person to wash up at the sink while another applies makeup at the large mirror.

OPPOSITE TOP RIGHT Light is a huge mood lifter; blending an abundance of natural and artificial light creates a bath space that is truly stimulating.

OPPOSITE BOTTOM When natural light is not abundant, opening up the master bath to an adjacent bedroom allows light from the bedroom to suffuse the space.

resources for "green" design

When it comes to residential design, green is the new black. In fact, the use of environmentally friendly, or "green" products and materials has become a top priority for a growing number of designers and their clients.

Fortunately, the bath is one of the easiest rooms in which to go green. According to the National Kitchen & Bath Association, an important part of what makes a bathroom green is water savings. According to the U.S. Environmental Protection Administration, a family of four could save more than 16,000 gallons of water per year simply by replacing a traditional toilet with a high-efficiency one.

There are many resources for creating an environmentally friendly bath that look and perform just as traditional materials do, and they cost about the same.

Going green is not just about what you put into your bathroom, it's about how you handle what you remove. There are charitable organizations that haul and recycle old fixtures, and many will offer you a tax write off for your contributions.

Finally, something as simple as buying from local vendors can help to minimize damage to the environment because less energy is wasted by packing and shipping items over long distances. (Think how much gas is wasted bringing that gorgeous natural stone countertop halfway across the world!)

Below is a list of green resources to help create a bath that's beautiful and guilt free.

◆ Green residential products and resources: www.buildinggreen.com

◆ Green products, safety tips, and personal care tips: www.greendepot.com

◆ Green information about the Leadership in Energy and Environmental Design (LEED) rating system, and other green resources: www.USGBC.org

◆ Supports charitable works and provides a tax credit by removing and reselling items being replaced: www.greendemolitions.com

◆ Green products and product reviews, water and energy savings tips, and more: www.SustainableSolutions.com

◆ Innovative and energy-saving light sources: www.wattstopper.com

◆ Topics related to green design: www.envirosource.com

◆ National "Green Pages": www.coopAmerica.org

ABOVE To create a master bath with maximum natural appeal, bring the outdoors in by taking advantage of existing views, making the most of natural light, and incorporating elements such as greenery and warm-toned wood.

liquid

indulgences

3

Water has properties that verge on the mystical. From the soft patter of rain on the roof, to the pounding crash of the ocean's waves, to the healing powers of a hot natural spring, water nurtures our bodies and touches our emotions, evoking feelings of purity, cleanliness, calm, and well-being.

RIGHT Where privacy is an issue, a delicately etched shower enclosure in a contemporary floral pattern doubles as a piece of artwork in the bath.

OPPOSITE Positioning the shower to take advantage of natural light from a nearby window helps to maximize the mood-enhancing aspects of the shower experience.

ater has no color, no odor, and no taste. Amazing, isn't it, that an everyday substance notable for what it lacks can transform a bathroom into the ultimate escape?

As more and more homeowners designate the master bath as their sanctuary for stress relief and relaxation, manufacturers are responding with all manner of ingenious amenities. The common denominator among these must-have upgrades? You guessed it: water. Whether it trickles, bubbles, or cascades from all directions, glows with color, or sparkles with light, water is the key to transforming the bath into a luxurious home spa.

SHOWER POWER

One of the hottest trends in bath design has been the evolution of the "super shower." Today's luxury shower systems, with their two-person capacity, multifunctional showerheads, thermostatic valves, body sprays, piped-in audio, and shower-organization systems, are designed to give the user a full-sensory experience.

In addition to its therapeutic value, the shower has also become a design focal point of the bath, with striking tile work and top-of-the-line fittings far too beautiful to hide behind

opaque glass. Today, clear-glass enclosures, some etched in subtle floral or leaf patterns and featuring very little metal or chrome, frame the shower fixtures and tile almost as if they were precious works of art.

Even the water takes center stage, with unique waterfall patterns, special lighting that makes it sparkle, and the option to program everything from temperature to water-droplet size. Indeed, showers have become so opulent they are increasingly referred to as vertical spas.

So, what's the best way to configure the perfect shower? Naturally, it all starts with the water. A single, static shower-

OPPOSITE Forget the tub. The newest "super showers" are technological wonderlands—fully programmable with every possible luxury.

RIGHT Natural stone is a wonderful material for creating a shower space with the feel of an outdoor waterfall.

BOTTOM Today's showers are far too beautiful to hide behind frosted glass. Here, a clear-glass enclosure allows the tile to make a striking design statement.

by
the way...

Time challenged? There's no need to waste a single precious moment waiting for the tub to fill up. Instead, just hop into a vertical spa. Today's luxury showers provide steam, chromatherapy, piped-in music, temperature presets, adjustable water jets, and plenty of hydrotherapy benefits.

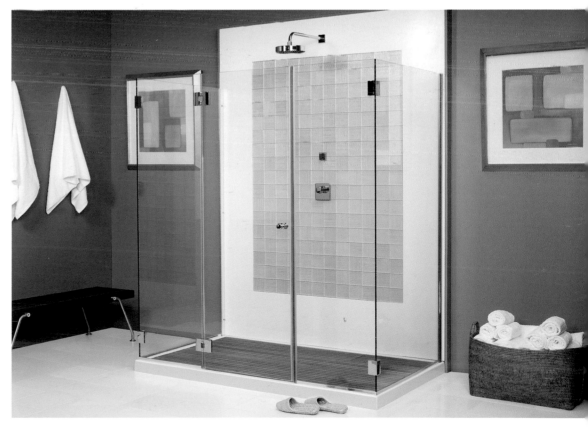

head may be functionally adequate, but why settle for just one when several adjustable heads can be so much more pleasurable? For those who want the massaging action of a whirlpool but don't have time for a long soak, body sprays can also be a terrific addition. They can be adjusted to "hit the spot," whether it's a sore back, neck, or other area of the body. And the experience of being hit by water from all sides can be the ultimate in luxury. To further personalize the shower experience, you can choose his and her shut-off valves and volume controls on opposite walls.

From a functional standpoint, a hand-held showerhead provides added flexibility, whether for rinsing off quickly, showering small children, or bathing the dog. An angled, built-in grab bar is also a must—and because it comes in so many designer colors and finishes, it can add aesthetic value as well as safety benefits.

A seated area—either a bench that spans the width of one wall or a smaller, built-in seat—is also a great addition to the shower. Think how much easier shaving can be with a comfortable place to sit down and stretch out! Nooks built into the

the shower has become a major design element, far too beautiful

wall for storing shampoo, soap, and and other products will also add convenience and help keep things organized.

In a bath with adequate space, a glass-free, open shower area can not only look great but also simplifies maintenance. Where this is impractical, frameless, clear-glass enclosures can maintain a clean, open look without taking away from the decorative elements inside the shower.

For those who prefer more privacy, glass block in curved, etched, and even personalized stained-glass designs can make a stunning, one-of-a-kind statement.

to hide behind opaque glass

OPPOSITE Watercolor blues are a perfect color choice for the shower. Unlike trendy colors that go in and out of style quickly, soothing hues of aquatic blue are expected to remain a popular choice for many years to come, according to the Color Marketing Group.

LEFT A spacious shower helps conserve time and water because it can be used simultaneously by two people. The TV, positioned to be viewable from both the tub and shower, adds another luxury touch.

ABOVE For the ultimate indulgence, a rain showerhead provides a truly delightful shower experience.

designer insights

Water is the ultimate indulgence—its flow, sound, light-reflecting properties, and fluid movement provide a complete sensory experience unlike anything else. Water is not only beautiful to see and lulling to hear, but depending on the temperature, it can soothe or invigorate, clear the mind, cleanse the body, drown out distractions, and provide its own little escape zone from the hectic pace of day-to-day life.

So, what's the best way to incorporate the wonders of water into the master bath to maximize that blissful feeling? According to designer Mollyanne Sherman, CKD, CBD, CID, of Newark, California–based MAC Design, it's about personalizing the space with the right combination of function, fashion, and flexibility, so that it's the best fit for the lifestyle of the users.

The following are her suggestions for making the most of the master bath's wet zones.

♦ People presume luxury is more about appearance than function. The reality is that a space that's flexible and efficient is the ultimate luxury. Focus first on how the space will be used, and make that as efficient as possible.

♦ If space is abundant, choose a separate tub and shower so each has its own zone. If the space is too small for this, consider eliminating the tub entirely and replacing it with a two-person luxury shower.

♦ When deciding on placement of the wet fixtures, don't be afraid to get creative. Just because the tub was always located in the back corner doesn't mean this is the best, or only, option.

♦ Some people love to place the tub in the center of the room to create a dramatic focal point. If this is what you want, don't forget about safety. Mounting a decorative tub bar on the wall will help prevent falls and make it easier to get in and out of the tub.

♦ To create a luxury-shower experience, multiple showerheads are a definite must! Plan to include at least one that's adjustable, located near a place to sit, with controls that are reachable from the seating area. Body sprays can also add to the water experience and can provide therapeutic benefits as well—especially if the master bath will not include a jetted tub.

♦ Soaking tubs can provide a spa-like touch, but for those with back, neck, or muscle pain, a whirlpool or air bath may be preferable. In general, water jets provide a stronger massage, while air baths offer a cleaner system. For the best of both worlds, consider a tub with both water and air jets.

♦ Showers and tubs are becoming increasingly high-tech, with multi-functional controls that can be located in a variety of places. While aesthetics matter, be sure the controls for all water sources are easily reachable from the point of use.

◆ If space allows, a completely open (no glass) shower provides for easier access and less maintenance—plus, it allows the shower to act as the focal point of the room. If this is not an option, clear glass can showcase a beautiful tile pattern in the shower. If privacy is a concern, there are a host of fabulous custom–glass panels that can be used to create a beautiful visual element.

◆ For those who are torn between their love of water and their desire to conserve water, a two–person luxury shower can provide the best of both worlds: couples who shower together save time and water.

OPPOSITE Forget all your preconceived notions about what a shower should be; the newest shower areas are full–featured rooms that are every bit as gorgeous as they are functional.

RIGHT Natural materials help to create a relaxing shower experience. Note the built-in seating area in the shower, which adds comfort and convenience.

JETTED DELIGHTS

While showers are getting more attention than ever, for many people, nothing replaces the soothing feeling of soaking in a jetted tub, allowing the bubbling, steamy water to caress the body and melt away stress. And these tubs have come a long way in the past few years.

Whirlpools of old had a couple of jets, usually located in a single area. By contrast, today's jetted tubs can have 12 or more jets that are not only adjustable but can be programmed to provide gradations of massaging action, from gentle to very intense.

As for design, jetted tubs are now available in a wide variety of styles, including Roman tubs; deep corner units with the look and feel of a hot tub, complete with armrests; huge two-

person tubs; and even freestanding clawfoot tubs. Whirlpools can fit into any design, from minimalist and contemporary to classic traditional styles. There is even an option for filling the tub through the jets, eliminating the need for a faucet that protrudes into the bathing area. Chromatherapy, aromatherapy, and piped-in audio are among the many extras that can be incorporated to create a truly spa-like package.

by the way...

Today's super showers can even get rid of little annoyances such as clogged showerheads. New rain heads feature rubber acetal nibs that break up calcium and lime impurities, preventing the holes from getting blocked and distorting the spray. These rain heads also work well in a retro bath design because they are reminiscent of the extra-large showerheads of the 1920s.

LEFT Create the ultimate super shower with multiple jets and body sprays, a separate, hand-held showerhead, and even a fireplace located nearby to add luxurious warmth.

RIGHT Contrasting a darker enclosure with a light-color floor provides added visual interest.

But even the simpler models often have plenty of amenities, such as built-in head, arm, and foot rests to provide added comfort. There are also a variety of tubs that offer heating elements contained in the tub's wall to hold water at a set temperature, so there's no need for refilling. And don't forget an ample tub deck to hold a pile of towels, a glass of wine, and a good book. There are even jetted tubs with built-in Internet access and TVs, complete with wireless connection, waterproof keyboards, and remote controls.

When choosing a jetted tub, one of the first decisions will be whether to go with water or air jets. Each has different properties, and each gives a different type of massage.

Air-jet tubs, which have made a big splash in recent years, offer a softer, lighter, bubblier sensation than the more intense water action of a traditional whirlpool. For those who can't decide, many tubs now come in combo variations—the best of both worlds!

SOAKING IN STYLE

Although less common than the water- and air-jet tubs, deep soaking tubs are beginning to turn up in more and more baths. These are generally smaller in circumference and significantly deeper than jetted tubs, providing easy, full-body immersion.

The great thing about these tubs is that they don't take up a lot of room, making them a good fit even for a small space. They also provide a way to literally retreat from the cares of the world, burying oneself right up to the neck in steamy waters that can feel like a heated spring. Many include chromatherapy to further enhance the feeling of escape.

On the down side, these deep tubs can take a long time to fill, making them less than ideal for those on a tight schedule. They also do not provide the hydrotherapy benefits of a jetted tub. However, for those who love that spa-like feeling, they can be a wonderful addition to the master bath. ◆

RIGHT Furniture styling isn't just for vanities. Note how the striking tub surround and deck add to the overall elegance of this design.

nothing replaces the blissful feeling of soaking

LEFT Curves are a wonderful way to soften the shape of a tub surround. The deck-mounted tub filler adds a feeling of luxury.

TOP RIGHT When creating a quiet bath retreat, simple is often better. Here, clean lines, warm wood, and elements of nature combine to create a zen-like bathing experience.

BOTTOM RIGHT Clean, modern lines make this bath a stunning showpiece. Note how the symmetry of the windows perfectly frames the tub, which acts as a striking focal point for the room.

in a jetted tub

therapy lessons

Sure, the bathroom has always been the place where people perform the morning grooming routines that help them look their best. But today's master bathrooms are designed to make people feel good, too, and as such, they offer a host of therapeutic benefits—from hydrotherapy to aromatherapy. These spaces can offer healing properties that affect all of the senses. Here's a rundown of what all these terms mean.

- ◆ Aromatherapy: Working with the holistic belief that certain scents can positively impact health and well being, this form of therapy uses a variety of essential oils—from peppermint and eucalyptus to lavender and jasmine—that are blended together to alleviate fatigue, promote relaxation, and even help manage pain. Many tubs now feature a small, deck-mounted well to house a canister for essential oils, which are heated and diffused into the air to provide maximum scent benefits.

- ◆ Chromatherapy: This form of therapy relies on the power of color to rejuvenate the body, improve the immune system, and evoke specific moods. Many tubs and showers are now equipped with built-in LED light ports, which can be programmed to specific colors of the user's choice or set to cycle through a sequence of colors designed to be soothing, uplifting, and mood enhancing.

- ◆ Hydrotherapy: Considered one of the oldest medical treatments in existence—having been used in ancient Egypt, Rome, and Greece—hydrotherapy relies on the motion of water to massage tired muscles, soothe pain, treat arthritis and other diseases, and improve fitness. Today's whirlpool tubs take advantage of this with a variety of jets that can be directed to specific areas of the body (such as an aching back) to provide a deep-tissue massage. Some offer several intensity settings as well, so the user can personalize the massage. Air-jet tubs, with their softer, frothier, bubble effect, provide another option for those with sensitive skin, or who find the intensity of water jets uncomfortable. For those who opt for a luxury super shower in lieu of a tub, body sprays provide the same effect while standing, offering "massage on the go."

- ◆ Luminotherapy: Because it's long been known that light affects mood, different types of light have increasingly been studied as tools for treating everything from fatigue to depression. With luminotherapy, intense light is used in the shower to help alleviate mood disorders, seasonal affective disorder (SAD), or just the midwinter blahs.

- ◆ Thermotherapy: This concept utilizes dry heat to soothe the body, relieve muscle strains, and stimulate the metabolism.

OPPOSITE
Today, tub fillers have become pieces of modern art. Even the flow of the water adds a mesmerizing visual element.

LEFT
Chromatherapy— the therapeutic benefits of color in the shower—is one of the hottest new trends in bath design.

BELOW
Neutrals are fine, but a bold splash of blue brings this bathroom to life.

If a long, hot soak is one of your favorite pleasures, don't be discouraged by a lack of square footage. Smaller, deeper soaking tubs and corner tubs can provide all the benefits of a luxury spa without eating up huge amounts of floor space.

OPPOSITE A deep soaking tub provides cutting–edge glamour and the ultimate in soothing relaxation.

TOP This bath may look like sheer elegance, but it's full of therapy benefits as well, with adjustable back and foot jets, a chromatherapy lighting system, and air jets along the bottom.

RIGHT An asymmetric design can create a striking, modern look.

vanity

flair

4

Nothing defines the style of a master bathroom more emphatically than a stunning vanity. Whether the room calls for an antique reproduction, a sleekly contemporary piece made of wenge wood, or a utilitarian model with separate grooming stations and dual sinks for him and her, the vanity sets the tone for the entire space.

OPPOSITE Mixing bold colors and dramatic shapes gives this bath its futuristic appeal.

BELOW Be sure to include plenty of storage options for items both large and small.

*B*ecause it is the major piece of furniture in the room, an attractive vanity is the obvious starting point in your master bath design. The vanity defines your space like nothing else can, so make sure that the piece you select reflects the overall feeling you are trying to achieve. Whether it's softly romantic, elegantly sophisticated, island casual, or Asian Zen, you'll want the vanity to be your first major purchasing decision when designing your master bath.

Like other choices you will make, there are no hard-and-fast rules when it comes to the color and finish of your vanity. Keep in mind, however, that dark woods generally create a more formal feeling, while lighter tones and painted surfaces impart a more relaxed ambiance. You can also apply stain or glaze to add depth and character to the base and choose from a variety of vanity tops to create contrast and a sense of elegance. For a more daring look, dramatic backlit vanity tops make the ultimate design statement.

Of course, what's inside the vanity is every bit as important as its exterior design. A well-organized vanity with customizable storage options will help you create a peaceful sanctuary by streamlining your morning routine and keeping each person's stuff in its rightful place.

FURNITURE STYLE

Nothing personalizes the master bath like a freestanding, furniture-style vanity. Unlike boxy, built-in units that look as if they came right off the assembly line—and probably did—these unfitted pieces give the bath a unique elegance.

Surprisingly, these furniture styles do not have to be expensive. While freestanding vanities are now available in a range of prices, it's possible to reclaim a favorite armoire or antique desk from grandma's attic for a look that is truly one-of-a-kind. There is one caveat to this suggestion: the humid atmosphere in a bathroom can damage some furniture pieces that were not intended for use there. If you own a fragile antique, it might be more practical to use the piece in the master bedroom.

Fortunately, many cabinet manufacturers are now offering furniture-style pieces with high-grade finishes that are impervious to moisture. If you want something with a traditional look, there are many vanity options with accents such as turned legs, fluted moldings, rope columns, decorative bun feet, beaded detailing, toe cutouts, and unusual toe kicks. While beautiful detail work can add character, more is not always better. These days, manufacturers are paring down the fussy, ornate details of traditional vanities to make them easier to maintain. This "less is more" trend also allows the simple beauty of the wood to shine.

While scaled-down details work best, that doesn't mean your vanity can't be eye-catching. Distressed or glazed finishes can add textural interest without overwhelming the space.

When it comes to color choices, darker woods, such as walnut and cherry, add a fashionable, formal appeal to the bath. Some of the hottest new finishes include deep mahogany, exotic wenge wood, and waxed teak—all good choices for an upscale look, especially in shades such as rich cocoa, espresso, or plum-tone sable.

If your master bath is less than spacious, you can move to the lighter side. A golden maple or white painted finish can visually open up the room, lending an airy feeling to the space.

OPPOSITE If space is limited, choose a petite vanity that is big on elegant details.

RIGHT Lighter wood tones visually expand the bath. Here, the soft color palette of the cabinetry echoes the flooring, creating a space that feels roomy and bright.

BOTTOM A freestanding armoire can provide additional storage for bath linens while adding a touch of polished appeal.

LEFT Bigger isn't always better when it comes to vanities. Instead of filling up this large space, the clean lines of this modern piece create an open, airy feeling.

OPPOSITE TOP A furniture-like piece with a vessel-style sink makes an elegant design statement.

OPPOSITE BOTTOM A floating vanity is part of a clean, linear design that's stunning in its simplicity.

CLEAN AND CONTEMPORARY

One of the hottest trends in bath design in recent years has been the movement toward open, clean-line spaces. This serene look is accomplished by paring down the distractions caused by too many ornate details.

As a result, there's been an increased demand for "floating" vanities that appear to hover above the floor, helping to open up the room's layout and make the space seem less cluttered. These European-inspired designs are often done in alluring wood choices, such as zebra or wenge wood, to add to the custom look.

Another major benefit of the floating vanity is that it's less likely to overpower a smaller space, even when you choose a dark wood finish. Decorative lighting can be installed below a floating vanity and, unlike a pedestal sink, this style provides both storage and counter space.

Vanities featuring curved shapes or modular cabinetry are another option for adding a contemporary touch to your master bath. Some even house refrigerated cabinets for holding chilled beverages as well as perfumes and cosmetics.

Another way to create a clean, uncluttered feeling is by choosing a vanity that provides closed storage, minimal hardware, and no glazes or embellishments. While simple is hot, super high-gloss is not. Very shiny surfaces are difficult to maintain, which defeats the idea of the clean-line look. What's more, shiny surfaces can create a glare that distracts from the space's user-friendly appeal.

Keep in mind that you needn't commit to either a traditional or a contemporary choice for your vanity. Today's most popular styles are transitional, which combines the best elements of both. What's more, experts expect this trend to continue well into the next decade. So, go ahead and mix turned feet with a bold splash of color, or choose a sleek, modular unit embossed with a demure leaf pattern. Just don't fall in love with beauty and ignore function. Open shelving can look wonderful, but unless you're committed to keeping it neat, this option may not be a practical choice for your lifestyle.

LEFT Cherry and maple aren't the only wood choices in town; here, pecan adds pizazz to this unit.

ABOVE A striking dual-sink vanity works as both a design focal point and a functional grooming station.

OPPOSITE Rich, warm woods with furniture detailing create a formal-looking bath environment.

HIS AND HER SPACES

To function at its peak, a master bath should have private space for each user. One of the best ways to create a truly comfortable and luxurious bath is to devise individual zones so that each user can get ready at the same time. Separate grooming areas prevent disagreements over who is taking too long at the sink, which partner's clutter is engulfing the vanity, who spends too much time preening in front of the mirror, or which party is responsible for the missing hair gel.

Ideally, you'll want to customize each person's space to meet his or her specific storage needs. This might mean deep drawers or multitier drawers with lots of little dividers; com-partmentalized cabinets; shallow, rollout shelves; jewelry niches; or an appliance garage for hair dryers and other electronics.

Different grooming stations also allow for installing sinks and countertops at heights that are most efficient for each user, even if one person is over six feet tall and the other barely reaches five feet.

Separate spaces can make everyone's morning routine less stressful, but both parties must play fair. That means an equal area for each user. Don't assume that because he's a guy, he doesn't need as much space. Planning an equal division of space from the start also ensures that one party doesn't feel inclined to "borrow" a drawer or shelf later.

the way...

Design your vanity space to minimize clutter and maximize organization. Drawer dividers provide a place for everything, from make up to safety pins, while pullout or rollout shelves make all your grooming products more accessible. An appliance garage—a clever idea borrowed from the kitchen—can also provide hidden storage for hair dryers and hot rollers.

different grooming stations allow for installing countertops at

heights that are most efficient for each user

LEFT In a spacious bath, the vanity area can incorporate abundant floor-to-ceiling storage, freeing space in the master bedroom.

BELOW This master bath's giant arches call attention to the various bath zones, including this stunning vanity area.

TOPPING IT OFF

Whether your tastes run to richly veined marble, rough-hewn granite, confetti-pattern solid surfacing, textured terrazzo, or sparkling glass, a vanity top should be a striking complement to the vanity base and add sizzle to the entire bathroom.

Marble and granite provide a fine contrast to wood vanities and, like most natural materials, are likely to remain stylish for years to come. Natural stone is also a great way to personalize your space because no two slabs are exactly alike. Remember that part of natural stone's charm is its imperfections—there's no guarantee that a granite top won't have the odd streak or color whirl, or a less-than-symmetrical pattern.

While stone remains a leading option, some people prefer experimenting with other surfaces. Quartz blends—a composite of approximately 90 percent natural quartz mixed with a polymer to seal the material and ensure stain resistance —have been growing in popularity in recent years. They offer the look and feel of natural stone, but with more color choices and pattern consistency and less maintenance.

Glass is also gaining ground in the bath. Its reflective properties help to distribute light and enhance the sense of openness in the room. Lighting can also be installed under a glass vanity top to create a stunning focal point.

Solid-surfacing material has long been a popular choice, particularly among those who want to keep maintenance to a minimum. It can be

by
the way...

Position the vanity to take maximum advantage of any light coming in from existing windows or skylights. Not only will this provide more light for makeup application and grooming, but the mirror over the vanity will multiply the light effects by reflecting it through the space.

BELOW A light wood vanity offers a feeling of warmth, while a black top provides dramatic contrast.

RIGHT Elegant legs and a curved front give this vanity a more delicate, stylish appearance.

fabricated into a vanity that incorporates a sink of the same material, offering a streamlined look and equally effortless cleaning. As a bonus, it is available in a nearly endless array of colors and patterns. What's more, its solid color is consistent throughout—unlike genuine stone, there are no "natural variations" that can sometimes look like mistakes.

Finally, for those who seek something totally unique, there are hand-poured concrete countertops. These can be inlaid or stained in a variety of colors and formed in waves, curves, or imperfect angles to fit almost any installation. ✦

LEFT A multitiered grooming station is ergonomically efficient and a good choice for users of different heights.

BELOW Drawer storage is becoming increasingly common in bath vanities because it provides greater accessiblity.

OPPOSITE Contemporary curves, echoed in the walls as well as the vanity, make a dynamic statement in this eye–catching bath.

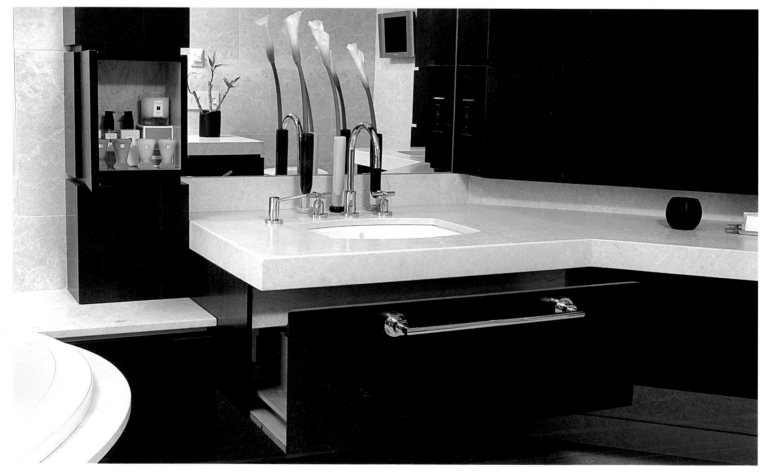

designer insights

The focus of the vanity area should be its comfort, style, luxury, and functionality, says designer Julie Howes of Cherry Hill, New Jersey-based Strober Building Supply. Following are her suggestions for creating a vanity area for your master bath:

- Consider how your space will be used. For example, if you and your partner are busy professionals, your vanity could be a no-nonsense spot for getting your grooming routine done quickly. For those who are able to spend more time getting ready in the morning, it might make sense to create an area for a coffee maker, a refrigerator, or even a TV to watch the news.

- Because the master bathroom is the most private space in the home, it's important for the vanity to address the owner's comfort needs, taking into account the height of each user.

- For an elegant look, furniture-style pieces can add beauty and refinement to the room.

- In two-person baths, separate his and her areas are critical. There's a perception that having a private area in the bath is more important to women, but women aren't the only ones who want luxury. His and her spaces should be equalized, which means that personalized storage should be incorporated into both and geared for the specific needs of each user.

- For women, plenty of counter space and a makeup area with excellent lighting are essential. Dividers can help to organize makeup, hair-care products, and grooming items. Deep drawers are excellent for storage, while drawers lined with black velvet can be used for holding jewelry.

- Cabinetry in the makeup area should include enough built-in electrical outlets so that appliances can remain plugged into an outlet. Check your local building codes first, however.

- For a good visual flow when the bath is part of a master suite, consider the furniture in the master bedroom when choosing a bath vanity.

- If the bath is small, consider moving the grooming area into a walk-in closet. This can significantly open up the space.

- A splash of color can enliven the bath, but avoid trendy combinations on the vanity that can detract from your home's resale value.

- Think of the vanity area in conjunction with the entire space; remember, you want a harmonious look in which everything works together.

- When choosing cabinetry, let your own personality come forth. If you're romantic, let your vanity reflect that; if you prefer an uncluttered appearance, choose cabinetry that fits into the design.

inside the box

A vanity's good-looking exterior may help define the style of your master bath, but what's inside is every bit as important. In smaller baths, storage space is at a premium, which means that you need to make the most of every square inch. For that reason, consider pullouts, rollouts, and even interior spinning lazy Susans to ensure that no space is wasted.

Compartmentalized storage is a great way to stay organized. Multitier trays with dividers can keep make-up, lotions, hair accessories, and grooming tools in their proper places, eliminating the need to scrounge around in messy drawers before you are fully awake.

Deep-drawer storage is one of the biggest vanity requests because it provides roomy space for larger objects such as hair dryers, hot rollers, bath linens, and toiletries. In smaller baths, a tall, narrow cabinet can provide additional storage without occupying too much floor space.

An appliance garage, similar to what is found in many kitchens, is another great idea for streamlining the morning grooming routine. In this case, one area of the vanity features electrical outlets for appliances that is set into a wall niche. This area is enclosed by a recessed cabinet door that slides down from above when not in use. Not only does the vanity look neat and tidy, but hairdryers, electric shavers, and other tools are protected from splashing water.

Finally, if you have a special jewelry collection, consider a door mirror that features a hidden compartment for valuables.

LEFT To maintain visual continuity, this vanity is topped with natural stone in a color that complements the border on the wall. A bright white sink provides contrast.

RIGHT Dark finishes are increasingly popular in the bath because they create a sense of richness and elegance.

BOTTOM Paneling the tub surround to match the vanity fills this bath with the warmth of wood. Here, extra storage is built into the back of the tub wall.

tile

style

5

From translucent glass mosaics, to metal that resembles medieval chain mail, to shapes that range from octagons to ovals, the latest tile choices are not your mother's pink ceramic squares. An array of new materials, colors, patterns, and textures allows almost unlimited creative options in your bath design.

One of the best things about today's profusion of tile choices is that you can mix and match less-expensive styles with pricier selections to create a custom look for your project without breaking your budget.

Tile is also a great material for creating a mood. Hand-painted tiles can be used in murals depicting anything from seaside retreats, to flower gardens, to scenic wonders from far-away places. A floral pattern can add a cheerful splash of color, while metallic tile imparts retro-style glamour. High-gloss, iridescent glass imbues the bath with a lighter, airier feeling. Granite or marble tile can be used to add richness, while travertine conjures an antique feeling.

Another advantage of tile is that it is easy to clean and maintain—and the latest advances in grout have gone a long way toward solving the staining problems of the past.

CERAMIC AND PORCELAIN

Although "ceramic" is often used generically to describe many kinds of tile, the composition of ceramic tile differs from other types. Ceramic comes from the humblest of sources: it is merely clay dug from the earth that's been fired at a high temperature to create a hard surface.

In its unglazed state, ceramic tends to reflect earthy shades in the brown-yellow or orange-red family, although it can be tinted with different minerals to provide greater color diversity. For those who love the colors and textures of nature, unglazed ceramic tile, such as terra-cotta, is a great way to add a rustic feel to the bath. Unglazed tile offers a matte look that is increasingly popular in today's "less is more" design climate. However, unglazed tile should be sealed to prevent staining and water absorption.

With its color, texture, depth, and shine, glazed ceramic tile offers a more polished look and a greater number of design possibilities. That doesn't mean that all glazed tiles have a glossy sheen; there are styles that have a matte or highly textured feel. Some glazed tiles even mimic other surfaces, such as fabric, leather, metal, wood—even wallpaper!

Porcelain tile has long been a popular option for the bathroom because of its easy maintenance and affordability. Unlike ceramic, the primary ingredient in true porcelain tile is finely ground sand processed under pressure at an extremely high temperature. The end result is a very dense, glass-like material with the same excellent qualities of glazed ceramic. Today's porcelain can mimic the look of other materials, including natural stone, metal, or even a variety of fabrics, such as the warp and weft weave of damask.

unglazed ceramic tile is very popular in today's

"less is more" climate

OPPOSITE Using tile partway up the wall, with a lighter color painted above, helps draw the eye upward and creates a sense of height in the space.

RIGHT A tile mosaic depicting themes such as flowers, fruit, or other favorite things adds a personal note to the bath.

BELOW Mixing shapes and sizes within the same color family creates greater visual interest, such as this bath's combination of diamond-, square-, and rectangular-shape tiles.

STONE EFFECTS

Tiles made from stone, such as granite, travertine, marble, and limestone, can be used to add a roughhewn, straight-from-nature appeal to the bath.

With its complex veining, marble has long been a favorite for bath surfaces. While most people think of marble in its high-gloss state, it can also have a honed finish for a more authentic look. Unfortunately, marble is prone to staining. While sealing can help, even a sealed surface won't repel acidic substances. For that reason, marble may not be the best choice for bathrooms that are used frequently.

Granite appeals to many homeowners because of its deep colors and one-of-a-kind look. Because each slab is different, granite provides character, depth, and dimension to many bath

BELOW Tile can be used to re-create the look of almost any material, from natural stone to leather and everything in between.

OPPOSITE TOP Oversize, rectangular tiles and a pebbled floor "mat" provide a striking complement to this sculptural, curved tub. The rough surface of the pebble tiles make them ideal for wet areas around tubs or showers.

OPPOSITE BOTTOM LEFT Natural materials and nature-inspired hues help to bring in the outdoors.

OPPOSITE BOTTOM RIGHT The shower is the perfect showcase to create eye-catching tile designs.

designs. However, because it is very porous, granite must be sealed to avoid staining, and requires that you seal it, again, periodically to maintain its pristine condition.

Limestone has a contemporary look and softly textured feel. This natural material, best known for its use in public buildings and monuments, has become prevalent in Asian-

LEFT Nature-inspired themes continue to dominate tile trends both here and abroad; look for honed stone tile that re-creates the feeling of a roughhewn garden wall.

BOTTOM Tile's versatility allows you to personalize your master bath with a floor pattern that you can design yourself.

OPPOSITE A variety of tile patterns and sizes in complementary hues create a wallpaper effect in this stunning earthtone bath.

by the way...

If you choose natural-stone tile, don't expect your installation to look exactly as it did in the showroom. Because it is produced by Mother Nature, stone often contains variations or "imperfections" that are part of its appeal. Additionally, depending on where the stone was quarried, shades can differ from what's on display in the store. If you're concerned about color matching, ask to see a sample of the actual stone that you'll be using before signing on the dotted line.

theme minimalist baths. Limestone is humidity resistant but stains easily, so it must be sealed to maintain its pristine condition. Additionally, limestone is generally softer than other natural stones, so extra care must be taken.

Concrete is another upscale option for those who love cutting-edge design. With the help of chemical stains, various aggregates, and colored pigments, a well-made concrete countertop or floor can look very similar to more expensive natural stone, such as marble, limestone, or granite. Another advantage of concrete countertops is that they can be cast as an all-in-one unit, lending a clean-lined appearance to the bathroom.

Travertine can make any bath feel like a Tuscan getaway.

ABOVE Classic black and white never goes out of style. This sophisticated master bath, with its coordinating floor tiles and tub surround, makes use of the latest tile options available in today's market.

OPPOSITE Geometric designs are among the hottest tile trends arriving from Europe. If you love contemporary design, consider a circle in a square or some other eye-catching blend of contrasting or overlapping shapes.

Travertine, a form of limestone, dates back to the construction of the Colosseum in Rome. It is best known for its texture and subtle color variations, which create a truly striking effect. Travertine comes in a host of design options, from polished to honed, tumbled to acid-washed, making it a wonderful choice that offers timeless appeal. Like other natural stones, it's prone to staining unless sealed and usually works best as floor tile rather than on higher-maintenance countertops.

designer insights

Unlike many other design decisions, choosing tile can be quite fun, according to Gaye Weatherly, a designer and owner of Weatherly Tile & Stone, Inc., in Portsmouth, Rhode Island. And whether it's textured subway tile or a stunning bath mosaic, she says that the possibilities for designing with tile are limited only by your imagination. Below are her suggestions for using tile to jazz up the master bath.

◆ To begin defining your personal vision, imagine what your bath would look like if money and space were not a consideration, says Weatherly.

◆ Select natural rather than synthetic materials.

◆ Flashy is out; soft and subtle are in. For a soothing bath retreat, consider natural stone and choose restful colors in the beige, aqua, and blue families.

◆ Select complementary paint in soft colors, and consider white woodwork and vanities to complement the tile.

◆ With the exception of decorative styles, tiles are definitely getting bigger. Obviously, you can't use gigantic tiles in a tiny shower, but if you have a large space, go with big tiles. Rectangular tiles in 12 × 24-inch or even 16 × 32-inch sizes create a very stylish effect.

◆ Look for tile with a lot of texture; this adds interest without overwhelming the room. Weatherly says she uses a lot of 4 × 8-inch subway tile in a wavy texture that adds depth and dimension.

◆ Tile is very versatile and has the ability to create many different looks. For instance, you can get a wonderful linen-like effect with tile in a creamy color that mimics the texture of real linen.

◆ "Beachy" looks are here to stay. Weatherly says she is currently using a tremendous amount of beach glass, which is a great way to bring the soft and soothing feeling of the seashore into the bath.

◆ Don't be afraid of grout; today's grouts are nonstaining. Epoxy grout is practically indestructible, and with hundreds of available colors, matching the tile is never a problem.

◆ In a shower with a frosted-glass door, there's nothing more beautiful than glass tile in colors that shimmer behind the finely textured surface.

◆ Don't be afraid to get creative with mosaic tile. Weatherly says that one beach mosaic that's absolutely gorgeous is sky blue marble in a wave pattern. Or you can do a beautiful cream tile with a soft aqua floor. Don't be afraid to experiment!

GLASS TILE

Because of its light-reflecting properties, glass has become an increasingly popular choice in the bath. Glass creates a less weighty look than other materials, helping draw light through the room and making it a great choice for those who want a brighter, airier space. It also opens up a small bath, creating the illusion of a larger area. And, of course, nothing creates the sparkle that glass does.

Additionally, colored glass can be used to compose unique murals, from beach-glass creations to stained-glass effects. Glass can even be backlit for a truly spectacular effect.

by
the way...

Today's glass tile is available in an almost infinite number of striking textures that range from iridescent, to metallic, to opalescent, to frosted. Glass can be a stunning accent in the bath, especially when it is incorporated into a custom border. A mosaic created of glass tile lends a clean, bright look to inserts, shower surrounds, and mirror frames.

LEFT Strips of colored–glass tile provide a dramatic focal point against an elegant marble backdrop.

OPPOSITE Iridescent glass tiles used in the octagonal inserts flanking this lavatory create a sense of glamour reminiscent of Hollywood in the 1940s.

OPPOSITE FAR LEFT Glass tiles in shimmery metallics are all the rage right now; the aqua tile here adds to the retro feel of this master bath.

OPPOSITE LEFT Tile remains a perennial favorite for shower stalls because of its cleanability, durability, and myriad style options.

OPPOSITE BOTTOM In this contemporary bath, high–gloss Italian tile adds a pearlescent sheen to the walls.

RIGHT Inspired by a stiletto's sharp edge, this Italian glass tile features an inter–locking design.

italian tile trends

Italy is famous for its fashion, furniture, and vast array of stunning designer tile. Indeed, some homeowners are so committed to finding the perfect Italian tile for their master bath that they fly to Italy to make their selection. So it is no surprise that the largest exhibition of international ceramic-tile trends is held in that country each year.

Fortunately, a wealth of Italian tile choices that incorporate some of the hottest looks from overseas is available in North America. These are some of the latest ideas for the bath according to the Italian Trade Commission.

MATERIAL CHOICES

In a country where fashion is king, it stands to reason that the hottest new tile trends incorporate elements from the latest textiles. These tile patterns—which mimic the look of silk, lace, damask, leather, and even denim—turn the notion of tile as a hard surface completely upside-down. The result is a huge variety of tile choices that provide the durability and easy cleaning of ceramic and porcelain with the softer, more delicate feeling of fine fabrics.

NATURE MOTIFS

While flower patterns are enduring favorites, the latest Italian tiles take a fresh approach to traditional floral design, with three-dimensional motifs, bas-reliefs, and tone-on-tone effects. Other new Italian-tile patterns are inspired by lush greenery and aquatic life, with ferns, leaves, and coral increasingly finding their way into many collections.

SHIMMERING METALLICS

Fashion experts agree that metallic tiles are the next big thing. Gaining ground in the kitchen, cool metallic tones and shimmering specialty tiles are also making inroads in the bath, adding glamour and sparkle to the grooming area in particular. In addition to traditional copper and silver, sleek new collections that look like oxidized metal, weathered steel, and platinum are lighting up European designs. In the U.S., metallic tiles add glitter to accents and trims. For those who love retro glamour, these shimmery tiles can transform the vanity area into a fantasy escape.

TURNING CIRCLES

While it might have been "hip to be square" in the '80s, today's tile patterns prove that it's hip to be circular as well. Just as curves are showing up on vanities, tubs, and mirrors, tiles with circular patterns are giving the bath a softer, less-delineated feel. Hot out of Italy are patterns that range from layered circles, to textured surfaces filled with tiny round dots, to circular cutouts and inset pieces. Hexagonal shapes that resemble honeycombs provide another interesting variation on this theme.

EAST MEETS WEST

Asian style continues to play a key role in bath design. This influence is being seen in Italy, where tile offerings include picturesque landscapes, delicate patterns, bas-relief woven bamboo, and textures that resemble origami, lacquer, and raku (a technique usually reserved for Japanese pottery). Advances in technology give these tiles a surface texture that looks almost identical to the real thing—providing easy care with a wonderful Far East look.

WELCOME TO THE JUNGLE

Animal prints are bringing a wild streak to the bath. Italian tiles with designs that mimic leopard and cheetah spots, zebra and tiger stripes, and snake and alligator skins are hot European trends right now. For more conservative buyers, these patterned tiles can be used as striking accent pieces in the bath.

FLEXIBLE FORMATS

Tile options that provide design flexibility are a big hit. This trend is manifested in Italian tile with a host of adaptable formats, shapes, and sizes that can be mixed and matched to create highly personal-ized designs. Hot trends include tiny, mesh–mounted mosaics mixed with overscale tiles, as well as rec-tangular forms in a variety of sizes. For more tile inspirations from Italy, visit Ceramic Tiles of Italy online or stop by a tile showroom.

RIGHT Designer tile options have come a long way from the simple 8 × 8–in. squares of yesteryear. Today, upscale choices come in intricate shapes, patterns, designs, and finishes to create myriad stunning effects.

a border of tile can demarcate wet and dry zones, separate his

SHAPES AND SIZES

Today's tile comes in a huge variety of shapes and sizes, from 2 × 2-inch mosaics to tiles that measure 16 × 32 inches.

Although your choice of tile should reflect your personal taste, there are some general guidelines to consider. Large-scale tiles tend to work best in a large bath, as they create a clean, streamlined feeling. With a small-size bath, a medium-size tile helps to keep the sense of proportion. Very small tile works best as a border, inset, or to highlight a specific area. When used over a large expanse, tiles that are too small can create a feeling of visual clutter.

While rectangular tiles are a big trend, square, triangular, hexagonal, octagonal, and diamond-shape tiles can also make a powerful design statement. Mixing and matching tile sizes or shapes also creates visual interest; for example, large tiles can be interspersed with tiny, patterned mosaic tiles. Just don't overdo it—the idea is to add a tile accent note, not create chaos!

Tile is also a great way to differentiate bath zones. For instance, a border of tile can demarcate wet areas from dry ones, separate his and her areas, or create a tile pathway leading into the bath.

Tile can also be a focal point, particularly when you use a unique tile pattern to highlight a grooming station, stand-alone tub, or shower. And with the growing trend toward glass shower doors, your beautifully

and her areas, or create a pathway leading to the bath

tiled shower can now be on full display. For added drama, consider tiling the shower floor in a different color. ✦

OPPOSITE A tile mosaic adds a stunning focal point to any bath.

ABOVE A tone–on–tone pattern, such as the one in this bath, provides textural variations on classic white tile.

by the way...

For those who want something truly luxurious, the rich texture of leather tile is a hot new trend. While leather tile is used more commonly in powder rooms, where high humidity is not a problem, it can also be used as a delightful accent in the master bath if kept away from high-moisture areas such as the shower or tub. Consider using leather tile to accent a grooming station or to frame a vanity mirror.

metal

works

6

aucets and fittings have become the newest baubles in the master bath. Once viewed as strictly functional workhorses, today's models sparkle with crystals and glow in finishes from satin nickel to oil–rubbed bronze. No wonder designers are dubbing this abundance of new hardware "the jewelry of the bathroom."

N ot only do the latest faucets and fittings add pizzazz, they play a key role in security, comfort, and accessibility. Stylish grab bars, showerheads that feature anti-scald technology, and hands-free faucets that utilize sensors for improved convenience and cleanliness are just a few of the hardware designs that are making today's bath smarter, safer, and more convenient.

STYLE TRENDS

Today, more and more homeowners are flaunting the formal, single-style approach to design in favor of a bath that best suits their individual needs. Happily, this mix-and-match aesthetic that blends different looks is easy to achieve, thanks to the abundance of hardware choices currently on the market. For example, you can incorporate a modern single-handle, side-mounted faucet into an Asian-inspired bath, or add a streamlined satin-nickel grab bar to a Victorian-era design. Whatever the combination, this approach brings together elements of new, old, and different worlds for a look that is both timeless and very much of the moment.

Incorporating different styles has a functional benefit as well. For instance, the beauty of an Old World-style tub filler can be incorporated into a modern deck-mounted application. The result: an elegant tub with contemporary ease of use.

OPPOSITE
Transitional styling incorporates the best of traditional and modern design, as it does in the sleek and graceful faucet here.

RIGHT A stream-lined faucet is the perfect companion to an artful vessel bowl and also helps save space in this bath.

Transitional styling has also helped to introduce a measure of minimalism into the bath, particularly in hardware design. While the cutting edge, industrial aesthetic so popular in Europe may be too stark for most homeowners, many are incorporating some of its elements by choosing faucets with clean, sleek lines. In true transitional fashion, however, these angular designs are softened by curves or mellowed by a burnished patina. Combining modern design elements with more traditional motifs in this way makes it possible to achieve high style in the bath without sacrificing warmth.

Other new faucet designs feature cylindrical or rectangular shapes for an ultramodern feel, while Zen-inspired, organic styles include waterfall spouts that deliver water in a thin, clear sheet. Large-scale faucets are also hot; they have a substantial presence and definitely update the look of the bath. Likewise, single-handle, side-mounted faucets look more contemporary, as do faucets crafted from a single piece of metal that are paired with hardware in unusual shapes or figures.

For those seeking a more classic feeling, Art Deco-style hardware may be just the thing. The retro appeal of a 1920s New York City hotel has been reinvented in today's bath faucets and tub fillers. The look is elegant and chic and often

OPPOSITE
A single-handle, wall-mounted faucet in a modern style blends seamlessly with Old World tile and contemporary glass, a transitional design that incorporates the best of old and new.

RIGHT **Mixing metal, glass, wood, and tile creates a cheerful and contemporary bath that is filled with color and texture.**

hardware is now less ornate, making it easier to clean

paired with lots of glass and high-quality chrome. High spouts and finely detailed finishes, along with crystal accents, accessorize the look.

Period designs, including styles reminiscent of old Italian villas, also remain popular for those who seek a sense of history and timelessness. These faucets have a tactile element to them; the way they feel is as important as their appearance.

In general, traditional designs are becoming somewhat less ornate. However, new approaches to tradition don't sacrifice form or function; they simply scale down the scrolls and curlicues. This also makes for easier maintenance because fewer details mean easier cleaning.

OPPOSITE TOP LEFT Today, it's possible to find a faucet to perfectly suit nearly any bath design.

OPPOSITE TOP RIGHT Accessories with unusual shapes, such as this hexagonal towel holder, add visual pizzazz to the bath.

OPPOSITE BOTTOM A crystal-studded towel bar adds a touch of sparkle.

BELOW Good design needn't be matchy-match; note how the towel holder has a completely different finish than the hardware and faucets.

WATER PLAY

Water is a living, ever-changing substance. Its sound, flow, and the way it catches light can be used to set a mood. And as the bath becomes more holistically inspired, water is playing a greater role in providing its ambiance. Whether you're looking to re-create a glittery, Hollywood-style retreat or a soothing, spa-like escape, the play of water as it flows from a faucet, showerhead, or tub filler has become the newest bathroom design element.

When water pouring into a sink is highlighted by a back-lit glass countertop, it creates a gorgeous interplay of light and sound. You can also choose a faucet that delivers the water in an unusual way, such as a rectangular spout from which water flows in a long, thin sheet. Likewise, a showerhead that twirls the water so that it catches the light can add sparkle to the shower, especially when lighting is placed at the water source. Some showers even offer multiple water patterns and droplet sizes so that you can have your own unique "water sculpture."

OPPOSITE Oversized, decorative shower-heads, such as this one, offer a rainshower effect and add a stylish touch to the bath.

BELOW A hand-held shower accompanies a wall-mounted showerhead, two must-haves in today's shower systems.

RIGHT State-of-the-art shower systems are growing increasingly complex, with rainfall showerheads, side jets, adjustable hand-held showers, and many other accessories.

by the way...

Intricately designed faucets provide a beautiful, upscale look. However, all those nooks and crevices require greater maintenance than a simple design. Likewise, a shiny finish requires more work to maintain than a matte finish, which is less likely to show fingerprints or water marks. If you're looking for low-maintenance hardware, think simple lines in a matte finish.

THE FINISH LINE

It wasn't long ago that bath faucets came in a choice of two finishes: chrome and chrome. But now that the bath has become such a prominent feature in many homes, hardware manufacturers have begun to provide more options in faucet design. Indeed, as the trend toward personalizing the bath has grown, so, too, has the number of finishes, with many companies now offering hundreds of choices.

Dovetailing with the movement toward nature-inspired materials are softer, more muted finishes that include oil-rubbed and Venetian bronze, and weathered metals such as wrought iron and aged pewter. Brushed nickel is another popular choice because of its durability and the way it complements a wide array of design styles.

All of these non-shiny finishes complement the trend toward using subdued, earth-tone colors and textures in the bath instead of high-gloss choices. The result is a rustic, warm presence that echoes the great outdoors. Another plus is that these finishes are less likely to show fingerprints or water marks, making them easier to maintain than the once popular shiny chrome.

Stainless steel has also begun to move from the kitchen into the bath,

particularly in loft or urban-influenced designs; while luxury finishes, such as satin black, rhodium, and antiqued gold, are popular options for upgrading the master bath.

However, not everyone appreciates the matte and muted look. Polished nickel and chrome still appeal to those who love smooth, reflective surfaces. Two-tone designs also continue to play a role in adding sparkle and interest.

For those who want something truly spectacular, platinum, sterling silver, or 14-carat gold finishes can turn the faucet into a gleaming piece of jewelry. Look for pieces accented with fine crystal to complete this luxe look.

OPPOSITE FAR LEFT Dark, weathered finishes, such as oil-rubbed or antiqued bronze, add a wonderful, timeless patina to the bath.

LEFT Bath hardware now comes in a wide array of designer choices, from simple white to stunning crystal, and everything in between.

ABOVE While the clean lines of transitional styling remain popular, traditional choices never go out of fashion.

RIGHT For those who prefer something contemporary, opting for simple lines is always a great choice.

WATER SAFETY

While water can be one of the bath's most beautiful elements, it can also be one of its most dangerous. For that reason, it's important that you incorporate key safety features, such as anti-scald technology and grab bars in the shower and tub.

Fortunately, the abundance of faucet choices makes it easier than ever to coordinate bath accessories for a total look. That means even grab bars can be snazzy, tying into the overall design scheme with an upscale finish that appears anything but institutional.

Include a grab bar in both the tub and shower if they are separate units. When a tub is located in the center of the room, install a grab bar fitted between two poles and mounted to the floor; this can serve double duty as an elegant towel rack.

To prevent burns and sudden temperature changes in the shower, look for pressure-balanced or thermostatic valve technology, both of which incorporate anti-scald properties. For added luxury, choose a shower that allows each user to "preset" his or her desired water temperature. No thinking is required first thing in the morning; just turn on the water and you're ready to enjoy your customized shower. ✦

by the way...

If you don't find what you're looking for in the store, consider creating your own custom faucet. As the trend toward personalization in the bath grows, some savvy hardware companies have begun offering mix-and-match custom-faucet options at roughly the same price as a standard faucet. With these programs, you can choose any spout, handle, or finish you like to create something truly unique.

LEFT From towel ring to tub filler, bath fittings help set the mood of the space and tie together the overall look.

designer insights

Faucets, fittings, and hardware should not only be great looking, but also provide durability, smooth function, and enhanced safety benefits in the bath, says Tom Cohn, Executive Director of the Bethesda, Maryland–based Decorative Plumbing & Hardware Association. He offers the following tips for choosing beautiful, peak-performing hardware.

♦ Buy the best faucet you can afford. Look for ergonomic function, as well as the quality of the materials, finish, and components.

♦ Pay attention to the warranty. The longer the warranty, the more confidence the manufacturer has in the product. Additionally, look at what is covered. Does the warranty cover the finish as well as the internal parts?

♦ Look for brass or stainless-steel hardware, both of which are more durable than products made of zinc alloy or plastic. Brass also offers an almost endless array of finish options.

♦ Choose a faucet with a ceramic-disk cartridge. Ceramic-disk faucets are nearly maintenance free and are generally guaranteed not to wear. The discs themselves have a diamond-like hardness; they are impervious to line debris, mineral buildup, and other common problems that affect valve life. They provide 90-degree turn technology, which means that the faucet valve is turned on and off with just a quarter-rotation turn. They also feature a positive stop, which means that the levers will never be out of alignment.

♦ Choose environmentally friendly products. Green is not just a fad; it's the future of design, so consider water conservation when choosing your faucets and fittings.

♦ Look for innovative sinks. A decorative sink or lav bowl can be the starting point for your bath design; the type of bowl you choose will dictate your choice of faucet, accessories, countertop material, and even the vanity.

♦ Invest in anti-scald technology. This is a worthwhile feature for shower systems and Roman tubs that enhances safety. Anti-scald means there is a sensor that reacts to temperature changes, thereby preventing the shower from suddenly getting very hot or cold if water is being used elsewhere in the home. Anti-scald technology is available in both pressure-balanced and thermostatic valves. Although thermostatic valves are the more expensive of the two, they allow the user to set temperature and volume control.

♦ Don't be afraid of radius technology. These sensor or "touch-less" faucets were initially launched in public restrooms with less than satisfactory results. However, the technology has improved dramatically in recent years. Sensor faucets are going to become more popular not only for their convenience and health benefits, but also from a conservation standpoint.

♦ Think twice about do-it-yourself installation. Improper installation can lead to costly damage or even flooding. In some cases, you can even void the warranty if a licensed professional does not install the product.

For more information about choosing faucets, fittings, and bath hardware, visit the Decorative Plumbing & Hardware Association's Website. (See Resource Guide, page 194.)

BELOW Frameless, clear-glass shower enclosures show off the latest shower systems, which are as sophisticated as they are functional.

RIGHT Unusual water-delivery systems, such as this sculptural ceramic spout, add visual interest at the sink.

by the way...

Wall-mounted faucets can make an elegant design statement while providing space-saving benefits. Be warned, however: because they are installed inside the wall, any leaks may not become evident until water damage is considerable. If you do decide on a wall-mounted faucet, be sure to buy a high-quality product and have it installed by a licensed professional.

buy the best faucet you can afford; look for

LEFT Forget honed or antique finishes in a light, bright bath and go for something with sparkle instead.

TOP A simple lever-style faucet works for users of all ages and abilities.

ABOVE Here, a butterfly crystal design inspired by Lalique transforms this faucet into jewelry for the bath.

RIGHT Warm, weathered finishes are increasingly popular in the bath, tying into the move toward nature-inspired spaces.

ergonomic function, quality materials, finish, and components

light

effects

7

When it comes to bath–room design, it's clear that the brightest solutions depend on light. The lighting you choose for your master bath not only con–tributes to how you see the room, but how you see yourself within the room. Whether you are applying makeup or drying your hair, you'll want the most flatter–ing view of yourself.

well-designed bathroom includes a lighting mix that enhances both aesthetics and function, providing a soothing environment that simplifies your daily grooming routine without detracting from the beauty of the space.

Whether you prefer stained-glass sconces, subtle recessed lighting, an underlit vanity—or all of the above—the right combination of lighting can help you look your best, improve your mood, and assist in preventing accidents in the bath. Design trends may also affect your lighting choices. For instance, the demand for higher ceilings in the bath has sparked new options, such as cove (recessed) lighting, chandeliers, and LED panels that set the ceiling aglow.

The bathroom is packed with an assortment of surfaces that may include tile or stone on the walls and floor, glass shower enclosures, metal faucets and hardware, wallpaper, paint, and window treatments. Because of this density of materials, it can be a challenge to coordinate a lighting solution that complements the various elements without distracting from the overall design.

Additionally, because the bathroom is a damp environment, there are safety restrictions on the installation and placement of certain types of fixtures. Finally, there is the issue of temperature control. Most of us want lighting that provides a warm ambiance. However, warm lights tend to produce heat—a characteristic that's not always welcome in the bath.

LEFT Multiple mirrors help to reflect the natural light streaming in from the large window in this bright bath.

OPPOSITE Large, square tiles provide a clean, striking backdrop for the graceful shape of the tub, which looks as if it is a piece of sculpture in this bath.

TYPES OF LIGHT

There are three main forms of indoor lighting, and each serves a different purpose.

◆ **General lighting** is the primary source of lighting, usually in the form of recessed lighting or low- or line-voltage downlights. Pendant lights or decorative fixtures can also be used as part of the illumination scheme. Note that recessed lighting tends to cast shadows across the face; never use this as the bath's only lighting source.

◆ **Task lighting** is designed to focus on an area of the bath where you perform specific tasks, such as shaving or applying makeup. Task lighting should be roughly 2.5 times brighter than general lighting, and is usually placed around the vanity, in a shower, or above a tub or toilet.

◆ **Specialty or accent lighting** is more decorative in nature and is often used to create a mood or spotlight a specific design feature, such as a hand-painted tile mural, crown molding, or a vaulted ceiling.

There's also the question of whether to use incandescent lighting (such as halogen) or fluorescent lighting. Both types have advantages and disadvantages.

Fluorescent lighting. Proponents point to fluorescent lighting's energy efficiency and its broad spectrum of color. Fluorescents are now available in compact versions, known as

OPPOSITE
Lighting—both natural and artificial—is a key component to any bath design, so never skimp on your lighting budget.

LEFT Swirled glass fixtures add a bright, cheerful glow to this colorful bath.

BELOW The color scheme you choose for your bath will also impact your lighting plan. Deeper tones will require more lighting than white or light rooms.

by the way...

Bulb selection is every bit as important as choosing the right lighting fixture. For lighting the vanity area, consider colored or coated bulbs designed to enhance facial features. White or frosted bulbs will help to reduce glare, while bath fixtures that cast light downward will help dissipate heat from the socket, thereby helping to increase the life of the bulb.

compact fluorescent lamps (CFLs), which can be placed in a wide variety of locations. What's more, it doesn't produce extra heat or cast shadows the way incandescent lighting does. However, these last characteristics also represent the downside of fluorescent lighting. If you want to highlight the texture of a stone countertop, the lack of shadow can detract from the overall effect. And unlike incandescent lighting, which creates a warm, softening effect, fluorescent light can be flat and cold.

While CFLs do come in dimmable versions, many people don't care for them in the master bath because they don't provide the soft, amber glow we've come to expect from dimma-

ble light. In fact, dimming a fluorescent light actually intensifies its blue tones, making the light seem cold rather than warm. The feeling of unease this produces is one reason why horror movies are often shot in cool colors.

Finally, there's the issue of how *you* will look. As anyone who's ever visited a department store dressing room knows, fluorescent lighting isn't the most flattering to human skin tones. Thus, while fluorescent lighting has come a long way from the days when it imbued a "Jolly Green Giant" tint on all it touched, most agree that color is still its greatest weakness.

Low-voltage halogen lighting. In contrast to CFLs, low-voltage halogen lighting gives off a pure light spectrum, making it closer to true daylight. It does a wonderful job of enhancing wood grains and colors, which gives the bath a more pleasing look. And because it's warmer light, halogen tends to be more flattering to skin tones. Halogen lights come in a nearly endless array of bulb sizes, which provide greater flexibility in choosing light fixtures. They also work quite well on a dimmer, allowing for endless variations of light levels based on mood or time of day. On the downside, halogen lights give off heat, and some argue that they don't work as well with earth or cream tones.

In certain areas of the country, including California, you may not even have the option to choose halogen as your main light source. With a focus on energy efficiency and conservation, some states now require designers to use fluorescent lighting as the primary source of light, aiming for a total ban on incandescent sources by 2012. It's likely that other states will eventually follow. Fortunately, this should be a driving force in creating better lighting options in the future.

LEFT Mixing a variety of different lighting sources, such as sconces, candles, and recessed ceiling lights, will help you maximize your bath experience.

OPPOSITE Specialty light fixtures transform the bath into an elegant, private haven, where beauty is every bit as important as functionality.

designer insights

Lighting not only plays a functional and aesthetic role in the bath, it also defines the space emotionally. The lighting scheme impacts not only how we see ourselves and perform daily grooming tasks, but also how we think, feel, and perceive the space around us, says designer Gary White, CMKBD, CID, president of Kitchen & Bath Design in Newport Beach, California. Here are some of his suggestions for using lighting effectively in the master bath.

◆ Invest in good lighting for your bath. Lighting is worth 50 percent of the emotional impact of a space for 10 percent of the budget.

◆ Don't let anyone steer you into a standard lighting design. The bath is not a one–size–fits–all kind of space, and your design should reflect your personal tastes, preferences, and usage needs. As a designer, the ability to do any style well is much harder than doing one signature look for everyone. The designer you choose should be able to reflect your vision, not everyone else's.

◆ Don't underestimate the value of adjustable lighting. After all, life isn't static, and your lighting design should reflect that. Create an environment that changes to suit your mood, the season, or the time of day.

◆ Work with a knowledgeable designer. Color and light are two of the most powerful tools to control

NATURAL LIGHT

Of course, there is nothing quite like natural light for creating a warm ambiance in the bath. Obviously, windows are a great way to bring light in from the outdoors, particularly if the light can be suffused throughout the room through a mirror's reflectivity or the use of a glass-block wall or partition.

Skylights are another great way to welcome natural light into a room. Both sunlight and moonlight create ever-changing properties that add to the pleasure of using the bath. However, they can also create glare. Using a white opal acrylic skylight instead of clear glass helps to diffuse and soften natural light, producing a warm glow that fills the bathroom.

OPPOSITE Positioning the tub to take advantage of a beautiful view allows natural light to cascade into the bath.

TOP RIGHT Large windows and a glass-block privacy wall help give this bath a bright and airy feeling.

BOTTOM RIGHT Good lighting is a key ingredient in a pleasing and well-functioning bath.

the psychology of a space. Consult with a professional who understands how to use those tools to create a master bath that will make you feel good every time you use it.

♦ Chromatherapy is about far more than just colored lights on water. It provides real benefits that can dramatically enhance the emotional value of the bath—and, as a result, your overall quality of life.

♦ Think of artistic light as coloring with photons. Texture, color, intensity, shape, shadow, movement, and pulse are all tools of this trade. Nothing maximizes the effects of all of these quite like a well-planned lighting design.

LIGHTING FOR LIFE

Understanding the difference between light sources is important, but you'll also need to know how to use each type to its best effect. For instance, if you shave in the shower or spend hours soaking in the tub with a good novel, you'll want the kind of illumination that best suits these needs.

Similarly, if you avoid turning on the light during a midnight visit to the bathroom so as not to wake your partner, or you have limited vision without your glasses, these habits might dictate a different set of illumination choices that add a measure of safety, such as soft lighting installed in the toe space below the vanity.

If you suffer from any kind of seasonal affective disorder, or simply get a bit cranky without sufficient daylight during the winter months, specialty lighting that simulates natural light may be a good solution. You might consider installing this type of light in the shower so you can enjoy your light therapy while you shampoo your hair.

Finally, there's the issue of personal taste: some people like very bright light, while others are more sensitive and may need dimmers to avoid headaches or eye strain.

the way...

Don't assume that recessed lighting alone is sufficient to keep the bath bright. A lighting plan should never be one-dimensional; instead, you'll want to layer your light sources to add depth to the design and help to reduce potential glare.

Whether it pours from a skylight or sparkles from a chandelier, lighting is a focal point in the bath these days. Of course, good lighting is critical in every room, but especially in the bathroom where you need ample light from a variety of sources for grooming tasks.

"Vanity or makeup lighting is always a challenge because you're supposed to get the light directly on the face to prevent shadow lines," says bath designer Gary White. "Most bathroom lights fire the light from above so you end up with parts of your face in shadow."

White also tries to give clients a multitude of lighting combinations that allow them to create different moods in the bath.

For natural light, skylights in the bathroom are an increasingly popular choice. For one project, White designed a coffer around the skylight. This was backlit with fluorescent lighting at night to keep the area bright.

Many designers also use solar tubes, which provide a considerable amount of natural light and are fairly inexpensive to install. "The reflection of light bounces around in the tube and into the room," White explains. "It's a very effective solution."

ABOVE LEFT A strip of lighting above the mirror adds a cheery glow to this vanity area.

OPPOSITE A variety of light sources in the bath will give you the best results. Include general, task, and accent lighting.

VANITY LIGHTING

The lighting that surrounds the mirror in a vanity area is usually the most important and hardworking source of illumination in the room. You will probably want to layer light sources here for maximum effect.

Placing sconces on either side of the mirror, between 30- to 36-inches apart at eye level, will provide optimum lighting for makeup application and shaving. Positioning the lights closer to the mirror helps bounce light onto the face, reducing shadows.

Sconces come in a wide variety of design options, from stunning stained glass to cutting-edge metal sculptures and everything in between. Choose fixtures that suit the overall style of the bath—or use them to accent an otherwise neutral room with a daring splash of color or finish.

Another option is to use strips of theatrical-style lighting around the mirror. Or use a halogen light above the vanity, which can provide good cross-illumination in conjunction with wall sconces.

Avoid placing recessed lights directly over the mirror, as these will cast shadows over your face that make grooming more difficult. A single open downlight over the mirror will also cause distortion and create an unflattering reflection.

Whether it's fluorescent or incandescent lighting, you'll want to use the same color and types of bulbs in the bathroom as those you use wherever you spend most of your day. You want what you see in the mirror to be a true reflection of how others see you in the outside world.

OPPOSITE **The light in the vanity area does the heavy work in the bath. Combining natural light with a variety of artificial sources helps to ensure the best conditions for putting on makeup and other grooming tasks.**

ABOVE **Coordinating the light fixtures with the faucets and hardware helps to tie the look together.**

ABOVE RIGHT **Each area of the bath, including the vanity, tub, and toilet, benefits from its own discreet light source.**

RIGHT **For optimum lighting in the vanity area, place light fixtures on both sides of the mirror.**

chromatherapy creates a soothing ambiance and adds emotional

WATER LIGHTING

Because the tub is generally the greatest safety hazard in the bathroom, effective lighting around this area is key. Illumination should be directed at the outside edge of the tub or angled toward the wall to avoid glare. Most jetted tubs also come with internal lights. If you enjoy unwinding in the tub, consider chromatherapy lighting for its uplifting effects.

Dispersed through the water, digitally-controlled LED lamps create a unique energy that soothes mind, body, and soul.

Lighting is also being used to brighten up shower systems, particularly in enclosed stalls. But this trend is not just about improving function. Chromatherapy is for showers, too. As with the tub, mood lighting is a great way to create a soothing ambiance while adding real emotional value to your time

the way...

When planning your lighting scheme, think of the bath in terms of zones, and light for the specific tasks that will occur in each zone. For instance, the area surrounding a soaking tub usually requires more subdued lighting than the grooming station.

OPPOSITE This simple bath highlights the soothing style and clean lines of Asian design. Add a shoji screen and bamboo accents, and you've got a Zen hideaway.

TOP RIGHT The pebbles surrounding the water in this soaking tub create the effect of an outdoor pond.

RIGHT Chandeliers are no longer just for the living or dining room. A gracefully ornamented fixture in the bath makes an elegant design statement.

value to your time under water

under the water. Sophisticated new lighting systems are programmable by color, duration, and intensity of light, with internal controls that enable you to change settings while you shower.

Light is also turning up as part of the water flow itself. Some showers and faucets now offer light and flow settings that create fascinating "water sculptures."

DRAMATIC EFFECTS

Lighting is a great way to bring drama into a space and create a mood. Fiber-optic lighting, which employs a remote light source, can create twinkling star effects when inset into the bathroom ceiling. Likewise, a shower ceiling panel can create striking light effects that change color with your mood. Stunning chandeliers blend light with dazzling crystal or stained glass in a variety of patterns and shades.

LED (light-emitting diode) lighting is also on its way to becoming the next big thing. Thanks to this new technology, homeowners can now choose from windows that look transparent during the day, but give off their own light at night when their power is turned on. LED wizardry also turns structural columns into cylinders of light, and can backlight tiles and wall panels.

Because it is relatively new, LED technology can be a bit costly. However, LEDs use so little electricity that they provide good value over the long run. Indeed, while an incandescent bulb can burn for 1,000–2,000 hours, a good-quality LED fixture can last as long as 150,000 hours. LEDs also offer low-heat output and tremendous design flexibility. ◆

LEFT There is no lack of glitter in this Hollywood-style bath, where unusual lighting creates the ultimate in drama.

ABOVE Pinpoint LED accent lighting creates a star-like effect.

OPPOSITE A skylight is the perfect addition to a nature-inspired bath.

bright ideas

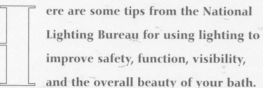

Here are some tips from the National Lighting Bureau for using lighting to improve safety, function, visibility, and the overall beauty of your bath.

◆ Light each discrete area of the master bath, such as the tub, the shower, and the makeup areas. Creating a scheme specific to the bath zone lets you have the ability to light one area at a time.

◆ The light in each area should be on separate controls. You want the ability to adjust light according to the task. If you shave in the shower area, you'll probably want to have more visibility in there. Lighting can also set a mood, such as a soft glow when you want a relaxing soak in the tub.

◆ You will benefit from lighting—especially in the makeup area—that emulates the conditions you find outside the bath.

◆ Light determines how you perceive color, and each type of light has a different effect. Consider having two or three light sources, such as fluorescents on either side of a mirror and halogen lighting overhead. An alternative may be a light-adjustable mirror.

◆ The lighting fixtures you select should be in keeping with the overall design theme. Equally important is to select fixtures that can withstand the moist conditions in a master bath.

◆ With few exceptions, compact fluorescent lighting (CFL) works well for most master-bath applications. The lamps are highly energy efficient and last about 10 times longer than incandescent bulbs. Buy CFLs on compatible dimmers. The quality of lighting is outstanding. Reducing greenhouse-gas emissions and saving time, money, and energy make them even better.

◆ If you are investing a significant sum in your master bath, spend a little more to hire a qualified lighting designer. There are many good ones who know how to use light to make your master bathroom both a showplace and a joyful sanctuary.

LEFT Decorative sconces can be used as accents, or to provide illumination at a grooming station.

OPPOSITE Light fixtures can add a delicate accent.

high-tech

they are still som
because the techn
market. However
functionality and
models, especially

OPPOSITE Progr
technological won

BELOW The new
showerheads built
ultimate rain–like

RIGHT Water, wa
let you aim the wa
customized experi

havens

8

any of us envision a warm, serene, and welcoming space when we imagine our ideal master bath. However, that doesn't mean that high–tech elements don't have their place. Today's cutting–edge bath designs incorporate a host of technological wonders, from mirrors that double as televisions to voice–operated faucets.

heating eleme

water temper

For the u

your master

fireplace with

the bath don'

an electrical o

Customizing the Shower

While the latest innovations have certainly improved the function and design of warming products and faucets, new technology has virtually transformed the shower. What was once a simple spray of water can now be customized to the owner's personal preferences, right down to programmable temperature presets for each user.

It all begins, of course, with the water, which can be pre-set not only to a desired temperature, but to a specific pattern

or type of massage, from soft rain effects to pulsing hydrotherapy and everything in between. Showers can also be programmed to combine light and color with the water for greater decorative effects. Today, even the size of the droplets can be regulated. If you enjoy singing in the shower, you can have audio speakers installed in the ceiling to provide a musical shower experience. You can even configure your shower to play music from your MP3 player.

Those who want mood lighting while they shower can

OPPOSITE TOP Steam technology adds a spa-like component to the bath.

OPPOSITE BOTTOM Now you can design your shower to suit color your mood, whether it's an invigorating red, a soothing blue, or a restful green.

ABOVE LEFT Why settle for a simple showerhead when you can have a shower filled with water jets or air jets?

ABOVE RIGHT While showers incorporate the latest, greatest technology, they can still be designed to blend seamlessly into a sophisticated scheme.

designer insights

As our homes get smarter, sleeker, and more advanced, that trend is carrying over to the bathroom. At first glance, it might appear that the goals of high technology are at odds with everything you want in your master bath. After all, when you picture a restful, soothing retreat, buzzing, blinking gadgets and gizmos aren't the first things that come to mind.

While it's true that most people don't want a futuristic space, today's master baths are incorporating technology to create a more luxurious, user-friendly environment.

That's according to Cheryl Hamilton-Gray of Carlsbad, California–based Cheryl Hamilton-Gray Design, Inc. She believes that the key to using technology successfully in the bath is to focus on amenities that contribute to the overall bathing experience, without sacrificing the warm and cozy feeling the space is designed to evoke.

Gray offers her suggestions for incorporating high-tech benefits into the master bathroom.

- Overall style trends in the bath, as in the kitchen, are moving toward more contemporary designs, clean lines, and sleeker materials. However, it's important to select high-tech elements that enhance the bath experience without detracting from the overall ambiance.

- Chromatherapy in the tub is a growing trend. Whether you want the therapeutic benefits of color, or simply enjoy how it looks, chromatherapy can make the bathing experience more relaxing, and it allows you to change the "mood" of the bath to suit your whims.

- Consider incorporating a towel warmer, which actually provides dual benefits. Not only does it keep towels toasty warm, allowing you to experience the pleasure of wrapping yourself in a heated towel as you step out of the shower, but it also looks luxurious and adds a feeling of refinement to the bath.

- While some people are now using warming drawers in the bath to keep towels warm, consider their practical drawback: towels pulled from a warming drawer will quickly get cold once they're out of the drawer, but a towel warmer will keep your towels heated until you're ready to use them.

- It's okay to mix high- and low-tech elements in the shower. For instance, Gray recently designed a his and her shower where his side had a rain showerhead, a standard showerhead, six body sprays, and a steamer. All she wanted on her side, though, was a hand-held sprayer. Today's technology is so flexible that it can be personalized for each user. Choose the technology you want, and let your partner do the same.

- Similarly, if you choose the high-tech bath route, the shower is the perfect place to begin. Look for showers with temperature presets that allow each user to put his or her ideal water temperature into the system's memory so that there's no fiddling around to get the hot and cold water just right.

- Don't sacrifice style for flashy technology. While there are some great innovations on the market that can enhance the bathing experience, avoid futuristic products that look

BELOW The newest techno-gadget in the bath is a mirror that transforms into a TV at the push of a button.

or feel institutional and detract from the overall design of your bath. For instance, some of the sensor faucets are interesting, but not stylish enough for an elegant master bath.

◆ A flat-screen TV is a great way to upgrade your bath, allowing you to watch the news or your favorite talk show while you get ready for the day. Likewise, an audio system with speakers built into the ceiling allows you to enjoy the luxury of your favorite music in the bath, without the dangers of dangling electrical cords. However, when incorporating electronics into the bath environment, be sure you have adequate ventilation so your equipment isn't damaged by moisture.

◆ Look for quiet ventilation options, including automatic venting systems that sense moisture and humidity and turn on and off without the need to flip a switch.

◆ If you love gadgets and gizmos, consider some of the "smart" shower options that can be programmed to customize your shower experience precisely the way you want it. Controls can be located inside the shower so they're easily accessible and don't interfere with your master bath's elegant design.

BELOW The newest techno-gadget in the bath is a mirror that transforms into a TV at the push of a button.

finishing

touches

9

The perfect master bath features all the luxurious amenities of a grand hotel—from built-in hair dryers and magnifying mirrors to stylish toiletry dispensers and uniquely styled hardware. Even the once-utilitarian grab bar has become glamorous. Indeed, the fine details are often what make the biggest impact.

*W*hether it's a built-in mirror defogger, a handcrafted towel bar, a favorite print of Paris, or a dried-flower arrangement that imparts a feeling of warmth and elegance, personal touches are what make the bath truly your own.

Just as you would pay careful attention to all the details—right down to the scented candles—when you try to sell your home, you should stage your bath to create an environment that is irresistible to you. Simply put, the look, smell, feel, and function of your bath should all be divine. After all, don't you deserve the same luxuries that you would put on display for strangers who might walk through your home during an open house?

Many homeowners think their bath project is complete once the fixtures are installed and the water is flowing. Instead, this should be when your true creativity comes into play. Now is the time to add details that will appeal to all your senses. Think plush towels, a dish of potpourri near the sink, an antique-copper grab bar, or a special mix of music designed for soaking in the tub. These components not only add to your bath's function, but they also act as subtle inducements that draw you into the space and help to soothe your soul.

OPPOSITE TOP
The faucet can be used as a sculp-tural piece that provides a unique focal point.

OPPOSITE BOTTOM
A narrow glass shelf can seem almost invisible, yet it provides some extra wall storage.

RIGHT For a clean-line look, keep the details simple; remember, less is more when it comes to accessorizing.

ECLECTIC HARDWARE

As noted in Chapter 6, beginning on page 106, decorative hardware can add a striking finish to the bath. Hardware, more than any other bath component, is ideally suited for personalization because it comes in a nearly endless array of choices. These can range from classic to contemporary, intricately detailed to totally whimsical, and everything in between. Designs can mimic bamboo, plants, flowers, sea creatures, seashells, animals, or just about anything else you can imagine. You can even select faucets or handles in the shape of musical notes or sports-team logos. There are stores that sell nothing but hardware, with literally thousands of choices. If you're searching for that special design to give your bath a custom look, stop by one of these showrooms and browse through the huge selection of offerings.

Today's hardware is also available with a wide variety of accents, including stained- or handblown glass, crystal, leather, hand-painted enamel, porcelain, or metallic finishes. There's also hardware created from authentic pieces of antique- or vintage-era silver or nickel flatware.

OPPOSITE Unusual lavs reminiscent of African drums are located beneath single-handle, wall-mounted faucets, adding a dramatic flair to this bath.

LEFT Dark, weathered finishes add nature-inspired charm to the bath. Look for warm finishes in everything from soap and toothbrush holders to towel bars.

ABOVE The mirror is a perfect place to make a design statement. Select a frame that's soft and romantic; complement it with similar-style accessories.

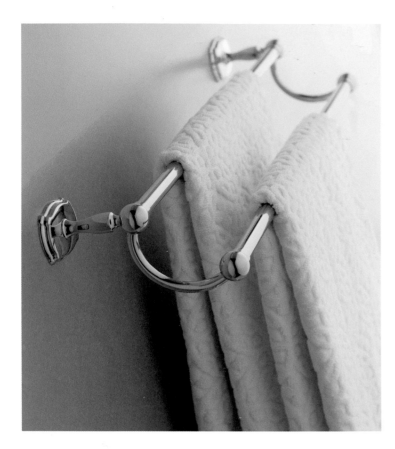

While shiny metal is still popular, the hottest hardware choices right now eschew the traditional look of highly polished chrome for a soft matte patina. Brushed and weathered finishes are hot picks right now because they blend beautifully with nature-inspired materials such as stone and concrete. Look for oil-rubbed bronze, brushed or satin nickel, antique pewter, copper, Venetian bronze, wrought iron, and brushed chrome. Stainless steel is also making its way from the kitchen into the bath, and many industry experts believe it's destined to be the next big design trend in hardware.

Although traditional hardware styles have become less ornate in recent years, small, intricately detailed fixtures and fittings can lend an Old World feel without overwhelming the bath with fussy details. Think tactile impressions as well as aesthetics here; hardware should be touchable, and texture will help to convey a sense of warmth as well as history.

If you're hankering for a contemporary look, keep the lines of vanities, tubs, and fixtures lean and clean—or opt for striking geometric shapes, such as a hexagonal towel ring. Leather is also a great contemporary choice for hardware—as long as it's kept out of the splash zone.

Grab bars, too, have become a trend statement as well as a functional necessity. Some designers have begun to install them horizontally so they can double as towel racks or mount them on tub decks for an added measure of style and safety. Look for grab bars in luxurious copper, rich, oil-rubbed bronze, or brushed satin-nickel finishes that add an elegant touch to the bath. You can even order your grab bar in a designer color, such as metallic lavender, to jazz up the look.

TOP LEFT For a small bath, choose double towel bars to multiply your hanging storage space.

LEFT This charming faucet incorporates the French words for "hot" and "cold" on its handles.

OPPOSITE A towel bar doubles as a heat source, warming the room while keeping towels toasty.

LEFT Nothing whispers elegance like crystal. Here, fine crystal is used as an accent on this towel bar, creating a high-end look.

ABOVE The right hardware adds the perfect finishing touch. Decorative plumbing and hardware showrooms offer hundreds of choices in a variety of colors and finishes to suit any decor.

OPPOSITE This medicine cabinet is cool in more than just its appearance; it doubles as a refrigerator that can chill medication, makeup, or even your morning orange juice.

ACCESSORIZING THE BATH

Just as the right accessories can make an outfit special, it's the details that give the bathroom its character and personality. Whether you're partial to funky metallic sculptural pieces or delicate, hand-painted porcelains, soft neutrals, or bold splashes of color, you can use accessories to give your bath a custom touch.

While mixing and matching materials is a hot trend, a coordinated suite of bath accessories can tie the whole look together. Most accessories now come in a wide selection of finishes to match the diversity of faucet choices so that creating a seamless look is easy.

On the other hand, if you hate anything that's too matchy-matchy, look for complementary pieces in the same tone, or use accessories to add a bold splash of color. Remember, accessories not only provide a host of functional benefits, but they also help to set the mood for the space. Choose pieces that speak to you emotionally as well as aesthetically.

As you choose your accessories, think about your storage requirements, including the types of things you plan to keep in the bath. Even in larger spaces, there never seems to be enough room

for the numerous items that accumulate, so stylish storage accessories are always welcome. Look for products that serve dual purposes and conserve space, such as glass shelves with a built-in towel bar or floor-mounted towel bars that include a toilet-paper holder.

If your shower doesn't have a recessed corner niche, shower baskets are an easy solution for keeping shampoo, soap, loofahs, and other toiletries. Hooks on a door or wall take up virtually no space while providing a place to hang robes or nightwear. If you take medication that must be kept cool, consider a refrigerated medicine cabinet. You can also store lipsticks, perfume, and other toiletries there to keep them fresh.

To dress up the vanity area, look for uniquely patterned soap dishes, toothbrush holders, and tissue-box covers.

Small accessories are a great way to add a splash of color to an otherwise neutral bath. For example, if you want a subtle look, opt for accessories in unusual shapes, such as a soap dish in the form of a flower or a wall-mounted toothbrush holder made of woven strands of metal.

Soap and lotion dispensers not only add style but they also help to keep the sink area clean and uncluttered. Dispensers are available in wall-mounted, tub deck-mounted, and free-standing styles in a wide variety of finishes to match any decor.

Built-in magnifying mirrors are becoming a must-have item in the bath as the baby boomer generation ages. These mirrors are perfect for putting in contact lenses, applying makeup, tweezing eyebrows, or any other grooming ritual that requires close viewing. For added flexibility, they can be mounted on articulated arms that can be moved forward or pushed out of the way when not in use.

The newest bathroom mirrors incorporate a special heating element that helps to keep the mirror crystal clear, no matter how long or steamy your shower.

ABOVE LEFT Unique sculptural wall art above the tub makes an eclectic statement in this master bath.

LEFT Copper grab bars add safety and beauty to this tub.

OPPOSITE Two-tone finishes, such as this chrome and porcelain towel ring, are popular for bath accessories.

by the way...

If you're going for a nature-inspired bath theme, be sure the accessories don't detract from that ambiance. Choose towels and linens in soft neutral colors and natural-weave materials, and accessorize with items that echo the theme: plants, coral, seashells, or even a pretty rock garden.

designer insights

Your tub, sink, and vanity choices may be the foundation of your grand master bath, but the finishing touches are what truly distinguish your space and make it your own. From heated floors and custom drawer pulls to multiple showerheads and personalized water-temperature controls, it's all about creating a private haven within your home that suits your individual style.

Achieving a satisfying master-bath design is as much about combining all the necessary fixtures, finishes, and hardware as it is about embellishing the space with small but meaningful details. In fact, according to Karen Dry, interior designer and owner of Westlake Village, California-based Garrett Interiors, Inc., the finishing touches are what make a master bath truly extraordinary. She offers the following suggestions.

♦ Plan lighting in the form of discrete zones, such as the tub, shower, and makeup area. Creating a lighting scheme specific to each bath zone gives you the ability to light one area at a time.

♦ Your bath should not only be pretty, but provide a deeply sensory experience, with each element helping to tie together that experience. For instance, when you think of luxurious bathrooms, you may imagine the soft, soothing sound of flowing water. However, a number of elements must be present in order to fully enjoy that water. These finishing touches include the smooth integration of lighting, the warmth of heated floors, and the incorporation of modern conveniences such as an updated faucet, piped-in audio and a flat-panel TV. All optimize relaxation.

♦ Personalize the space with details that support how you live. If you like hot coffee in the morning, incorporate a tiny kitchenette into the space. If you have special storage needs for jewelry or makeup, make sure there is an ample area for this, and include inventive storage solutions that maximize every available corner. Above all, design your bath with your needs in mind.

♦ Be brave! Even if you're conservative in other areas of the home, you can incorporate some "wow" details into the bath. These can be as simple as turning something ordinary into something extraordinary, such as mounting a faucet on a pedestal or on the wall, opting for a laser-sensor faucet, or designing a creative tile pattern.

♦ Flexibility can mean the difference between a good bath and a great one. For instance, having task, ambient, and decorative lighting installed so that each type can be controlled independently allows you to use the bath the way you choose at any time of day or night.

♦ Pay special attention to dressing and bathing areas, and incorporate special details, such as a favorite framed print, that will help enhance the feeling of a private, luxurious retreat.

♦ Don't just replace what you currently have with the same old thing. Every day, new and innovative products are being introduced that provide a wealth of options for making your bath truly special.

RIGHT Seashells used on the mirror frame and displayed on the shelves add a striking finishing touch to this vanity area design.

by
the way...

Accessorize your space with things that have meaning to you: beach glass collected from long walks on the shore, framed photos of favorite vacation spots, or a collection of perfume bottles can make the bath a more intimate and enjoyable place in which to spend time.

DECORATIVE TOUCHES

Once you've decided on all the essentials, it's time to indulge in a few purely aesthetic details. These can be as simple or as decadent as your tastes dictate, from handwoven towels to a rock garden with a burbling fountain and forest-like sound effects.

When putting together these finishing touches, consider the theme of your bath. For instance, if you're going for a beachy, cottage-by-the-sea feel, use pretty shells or starfish in a variety of shapes and sizes as decorative elements. If your bath is more Tuscany villa in style, a painted mural on one wall can be a wonderful way to add a bit of Old World charm. To dress up a Zen-like bath, add a shoji screen and bamboo accents. For a glamorous Art Deco bath, consider an ornate, oversized mirror over the vanity area to re-create the feeling of a Hollywood star's dressing room.

If your bath doesn't have a specific theme, think about what fits the space. If the design is soft and romantic, gracefully draped window treatments and dried-flower arrangements may be the perfect accoutrements. If the design is more contemporary, a simple, wall-hung sculpture could be just the right touch to accent the space.

Fresh flowers, small potted plants, or artwork can also help to dress up the bath. Or go with something more personal, such as polished stones you collected on the beach, a framed photograph of the sunset you enjoyed on your Alaskan cruise, or small figurines you picked up in Madrid. All can help to make the space feel more inviting.

Bath towels can also play a key role in your comfort and enjoyment. After all, what good is a supershower with all the bells and whistles if you dry off with a skimpy towel?

RIGHT Finishing the bath isn't just about adding things, it's about choosing components that blend to create a beautiful, cohesive whole.

fresh flowers, small plants, a collection of polished stones,

or a framed photograph all help to personalize your bath

When remodeling your bath, splurge on new linens in plush, top-of-the-line materials or monogrammed hand towels to set off that striking new towel bar.

Towels can be used to add a splash of color to the bath, but be sure not to go overboard; many a nature-inspired bath has been ruined by a jarringly bright towel made of synthetic material.

SCENT-SATIONS

Because a truly great master bath provides a full sensory experience, it's important that the finishing touches take into account not only each sense, but also each scent. Indeed, of the five senses, smell is the one most closely tied to memory and imagination. It makes sense to create a private retreat that includes plenty of positive scent-sations.

Fragrance candles, scented soaps, potpourri, and aromatic oils can all be incorporated into the bath. Depending on the feeling you want to evoke, you might choose herbaceous lavender, soothing chamomile, or energizing peppermint, or vary the scents according to your mood. Potted herbs, such as peppermint lend scent appeal, and plants, such as aloe, offer benefits for minor skin irritations as well. ✦

by the way...

As you accessorize, don't just think about visuals. Your bath retreat should provide a full sensory experience. Consider tactile impressions, scents, and even sounds. Perhaps a piece of sculpture containing a waterfall or a bubbling saltwater fish tank would be the perfect touch for completing your bath.

suite

sensations

10

Can you imagine the luxury of an *ensuite* space where you can exercise, brew your morning coffee, take a blissful tub soak, and select the day's attire? A master–bath suite is the ultimate sanctuary, complete with sitting area, walk-in closet, kitchen—even a spot for doing yoga poses— before you face the demands of the day.

BELOW Do away with doors and use archways and skylights for a light-filled, seamless flow between spaces.

OPPOSITE Your master-bath suite might include an upholstered window seat with some cushy throw pillows or a comfortable couch for curling up with a good book.

*O*f course, you will need a bit of dedicated space in order to create a truly grand master suite. But that doesn't necessarily mean building a costly extension to your house. Is your bedroom adjacent to a home office you hardly use? Armed with a laptop, you can work nearly anywhere, but most people need a private place in order to rest and relax. Perhaps this room would better fit your needs if it was allocated to a large master suite. Likewise, if you still preserve your kid's bedroom—even though she now has kids of her own—it might be time to convert this space into something more useful. And why keep your bath linens stashed in a hall closet when you can incorporate this square footage into a bath suite with plenty of storage?

Because it encompasses the two most private rooms in the home—the bedroom and the bathroom—the master suite is obviously a very personal place. For this reason, you should never submit to a standard, cookie-cutter design. Rather, the components of the master suite should be determined by your bathing and grooming routines, daily schedule, organizational habits, relaxation methods, style preferences, and overall lifestyle factors.

Consider what your morning routine is actually like now, as opposed to what you would really prefer. Do you stumble around in the dark, trying to find an outfit to wear without waking your spouse? Or are you constantly digging shoes out from under the bed? A separate dressing room where you can mix and match clothing and line up your shoes by color might be the solution.

Do you shower in three minutes flat, or do you prefer to soak in the tub until your body revs up? If it's the latter, a tub with energizing chromatherapy might be on your wish list.

Does your treadmill sit in the basement, doing little more than serve as a substitute clothes hanger? Perhaps moving it closer to where you spend time every morning is the motivation you need to finally get that fitness routine going.

Remember, the key to creating the master suite of your dreams is to design a space that will help you to be your best. If that means having at least your first cup of coffee before facing the kids or doing 30 minutes of yoga before bed, then plan your space to accommodate these needs.

THE BATH SUITE

The plan for your master suite should begin with the bathroom space. When you conceive your bath layout, it's a good idea to separate wet and dry areas and divide the bath into specific zones according to function. Be sure each area offers a modicum of privacy. A separate toilet compartment, dual grooming stations, and a large shower—placed far enough away from the vanity to avoid steaming up the mirror—will provide dedicated areas for each user to enjoy privacy, even if both people are occupying the space. An equally important result of this plan is the serene, uncluttered atmosphere you will create.

Think about incorporating "living room" features into your master-bath suite, such as an upholstered sofa, chair, or fabric-covered bench, a fireplace, framed art work, and a flatscreen television. Think opulent: the idea is to create a space that's not just for bathing, but also for relaxing.

High or vaulted ceilings will make the space feel larger and more inviting. Be sure to keep the color scheme warm, though; large spaces need soft colors and plenty of texture to help them feel comfortable and inviting. Draped fabric can also help to create a sense of warmth and elegance, while also muffling unpleasant echoes. Coordinating fabrics can be used to accent windows, add interest to walls or archways, or to frame a tub.

Wide doorways not only make the space more accessible, they create a more open feeling between the bathroom and adjoining spaces. This is especially valuable if the bath doesn't contain windows; opening up the space between the bath and the other rooms can help transmit natural light from the bedroom into the bath.

by the way...

If you love to end your day with a hot bath and some chilled chardonnay, or a romantic toast with a glass or two of dry champagne, consider adding a wine cooler to your master suite. The newest units look like furniture and add the perfect touch of luxury for those days when you want to escape from it all without ever leaving home.

LEFT Does your bath lack a dramatic view? You can create your own. This bath features indoor greenery, Asian-inspired design, and comfortable seating for enjoying the ambiance.

OPPOSITE When a space is too small for a separate sitting room, tuck a comfortable upholstered chair into the bath to create a spot to rest for a moment.

THE SITTING ROOM

While many master baths contain a makeup or grooming area apart from the wet zones, a private sitting room is a truly pampering feature. There's something delightfully decadent about a space devoted completely to relaxation, so it's perfectly acceptable to take a sybaritic approach to its design.

For a space with a romantic feel, look for silks, satins, and chiffons that drape and flow. If you prefer something more tailored, look for natural fabrics with plenty of texture or rich, butter-soft leather that is inviting to touch.

Make sure your seating area is not only comfortable but well lit; this could become your favorite spot for curling up with a book. And don't forget a fireplace for winter mornings!

By separating the grooming area from the moisture-filled tub and shower, you create many additional design possibilities, from a wall display of photographs and artwork to shelves filled with books to a tapestry-covered club chair and ottoman, complete with silk throw pillows. Because there is no concern about humidity, there are few decorating restrictions.

As a private space, the sitting room is perfect for personalizing, whether it's a collection of porcelain dolls, valuable sports memorabilia, or a display cabinet that shows off crystals or other collectibles.

Be sure to include some scented candles or aromatic plants to enhance the ambiance, along with lighting on a dimmer so you change the mood with the flip of a switch.

OPPOSITE
An elegant, furniture-style vanity is complemented by a feminine chair, giving this bath suite the air of a drawing room.

RIGHT A fireplace in the master-bath suite is the ultimate luxury. Locate it near the tub for a cozy, romantic ambiance.

the way...

Windows in a dressing area provide natural light and a beautiful view. But direct and prolonged exposure to sunlight can fade shoes and clothing. If you do have windows, be sure to cover them with sunlight-filtering shades, and store clothes and shoes away from strong sunlight.

BELOW A lav and TV tucked into the handsome wood cabinetry in this dressing area represent true luxury.

BELOW RIGHT A jewelry tray in the dressing area keeps favorite pieces nearby for matching the day's outfit.

OPPOSITE A complete dressing suite makes choosing your outfit a pleasure. Seating beneath a window is the perfect place for contemplating the day's attire.

THE WALK-IN CLOSET

An expansive area for storing clothes is another key component of the luxury master suite. A separate dressing area limits clutter and results in a more serene sleeping space. In fact, many people who have walk-in closets swear that their bedrooms feel bigger because they are no longer filled with piles of laundry, shoes left by the bed, and the like.

Another bonus of a walk-in closet is that you can personalize the space to suit your lifestyle. For example, if you own more shoes than you can possibly wear, you can dedicate an entire wall to shoe racks or shelving. If your taste runs to cashmere sweaters, you can have rows of sweater compartments to keep each item neatly folded and accessible. The fashionista can indulge her shopping habit with extra hanging space for her large collection of dresses, jeans, and handbags.

For the ultimate in personalization, some closet companies offer online programs that allow you to design your own closet on your computer, based on data that includes your height, the available square footage, and the type and amount of storage you need. These closet systems can be obtained at nearly any price point, from high-end, furniture-style closets with elaborate wood moldings and beautifully crafted fittings to simpler creations in laminate with chrome or wire interiors.

THE DRESSING ROOM

While a walk-in closet is a wonderful addition to the master-bath suite, for those who have the space, a dressing room is the ultimate treat. Basically an expanded walk-in closet, a dressing room often features a furniture-style island or seating area, a well-lit grooming station, a full-length mirror, and copious space for clothing storage that may include hanging racks, shelves, compartments, a dresser, or all of the above.

Unlike a closet, a dressing room is designed to be seen and enjoyed, so this is a great place to include furniture and decorative elements such as crown molding, wood paneling, elegant hardware, and sumptuous upholstery. You can design a space specific to your needs or buy premade wall systems that feature multiple storage options.

Because this is where you will get dressed, it's also a good idea to include a steamer, ironing board, or other appliances that remove wrinkles and help keep clothing in tip-top condition. Some people also choose to include a hamper tucked out of sight, along with a washer and dryer that are paneled to match the furniture. This keeps laundry close to where it's stored—a terrific time saver!

Typically, you'll want to allow a 16- to 18-inch depth for shelves that hold folded clothing. Hanging rods should be layered at 40 inches and 80 inches above the floor to allow space for shorter items, such as blouses, and longer items, such as dresses or pants. However, also consider your own height—someone who is shorter than average may find 80 inches too high to easily reach clothing and other items.

For those who prefer to take their time getting dressed, a flat-screen television is a welcome addition for watching a favorite morning show while getting ready for the day. And if you simply can't function without checking your e-mail first thing in the morning, a dressing room might incorporate a laptop charging station so your mail is readily available.

BELOW If you have the square footage, plan a sumptuous dressing area with copious storage space, a sit–down grooming area, and a center island for holding folded sweaters and accessories.

ABOVE LEFT A valet tray provides a fail–safe drop spot for glasses, cell phone, keys, and cologne.

ABOVE CENTER Dividers maximize drawer space and keep your things perfectly organized.

RIGHT Narrow pullout columns can be used for ties, cufflinks, sunglasses, and other small items.

THE BREAKFAST BAR

If you can barely stumble into the bathroom before your morning coffee kicks in, why not incorporate a breakfast bar into your master suite? A "morning kitchen," as they're frequently called, takes up minimal space yet allows you to start your day with hot coffee, a cold glass of juice, or a toasted English muffin. A small kitchen also makes it easy to indulge in a glass of wine or a light snack while soaking in your whirlpool or grab a cold drink after your morning exercises.

Designate one area in the bedroom, dressing room, or grooming area for a minifridge, microwave, toaster oven, and programmable coffeemaker. This way, your coffee will be brewing when your alarm goes off—and the aroma may make it easier to get out of bed.

If your bedroom isn't as large as you'd like, a refrigerated drawer can be a space-saving, flexible option. Likewise, locating your breakfast bar next to a dresser or vanity provides an easy landing spot without the need for a separate eating area.

If space is more abundant, you can add overhead cabinetry for additional snacks or glassware, a wine cooler for romantic nights, or a cozy window seat so you can enjoy breakfast overlooking a pretty view.

THE EXERCISE AREA

A workout space is the hottest new amenity turning up in the master-bath suite. As with real estate, it's all about location: exercise is hard enough without having to drag yourself down to the basement. However, a small, dedicated area just steps away from the shower or sauna makes a morning yoga or treadmill session much more inviting.

While this may seem like an impossible extravagance, especially if space is

space for exercise

Are you thinking of incorporating a gym into your master suite, but don't know how much space you'll need? While it's always a good idea to measure equipment before you buy, the San Diego, California-based American Council on Fitness offers these space guidelines

- ◆ Treadmills — 30 square feet
- ◆ Single-Station Gym — 35 square feet
- ◆ Free Weights — 20–50 square feet
- ◆ Bikes — 10 square feet
- ◆ Rowing Machines — 20 square feet
- ◆ Stair-climbers — 10–20 square feet
- ◆ Ski Machines — 25 square feet
- ◆ Multi-Station Gym — 50–200 square feet

OPPOSITE A compact morning kitchen with double refrigerated drawers is perfect for enjoying a light breakfast, glass of juice, or an early morning cup of coffee or tea.

BELOW Installing exercise equipment near the bath and grooming area increases the likelihood of regular workouts.

tight, a simple exercise area requires little more than a mat and enough space for stretching, pilates, aerobics, or weight lifting. A wall-mounted television to play exercise videos can finish off the space.

If square footage is not a problem, you can incorporate a treadmill, free weights, a stationery bike, stair-climber machine, weight stations, or other equipment. A high-end audio system is a great addition, along with storage for the music CDs that help to get you moving.

When planning for an exercise area, avoid hanging light fixtures too low, which can be a hazard, and look for cushioned floor mats that filter out noise. A small closet can also provide storage space for a fold-away treadmill, mats, weights, and other equipment. And for an added touch of luxury, consider incorporating a sauna to soothe your muscles and relax your mind after a tough workout. ◆

designer insights

The master-bath suite is the ultimate luxury, combining beauty, function, technology, organization, and restful indulgence. Designer Julie Stoner, ASID, CKD, of the Boca Raton, Florida-based Kitchen & Bath Galleria, shares her thoughts on how to create a grand master-bath suite.

◆ The luxury bath suite creates a truly decadent experience; so if you're going to splurge, this is the place to do it. To be able to stand in a spacious shower and enjoy the warmth of a cozy fireplace while watching the news on a flat-panel television is a true indulgence.

◆ The most important element in the master bath is a private area for the toilet. The shower, also separate, should incorporate a view to the lounging area. Privacy and the ability to close doors when you choose to is key.

◆ Be sure the makeup and grooming area is removed from steam or moisture from the shower area, and keep his and her areas separate to afford everyone some morning privacy.

◆ Mix warm elements (live plants, a cozy fireplace) with high-tech ones (piped-in audio, a television) to create a restful yet multifunctional space.

◆ Take advantage of outside views. For instance, a whirlpool bath overlooking the garden creates a wonderful ambiance.

◆ Choose a monochromatic or tone-on-tone color scheme in blush or neutral shades that complement skin tones. These create a harmonious, serene feeling that meshes well with the calm, relaxed feeling you hope to achieve in the space.

◆ Consider attractive bench seating and a lovely tile pattern in the shower to make the experience more relaxing.

◆ Compartmentalize areas by zone or function. However, be sure that each space flows well with the others. When you step into the bath suite, you want to be cocooned within a calm, soothing retreat—not one that leaves you feeling uncomfortable.

◆ For a wonderfully luxurious touch, consider including a sitting room adjacent to the bath where you can snuggle up and read.

◆ Plan space for a large closet, perhaps with separate his and her areas, where everything is compartmentalized. Use hanging racks, high racks, and drawers to separate lingerie, sweaters, shoes, and accessories. You can also incorporate pullout wall storage, hamper pullouts, tie and belt racks, and wicker baskets.

◆ Compartmentalized closet systems don't have to be laminate, cookie-cutter designs. Instead, you can achieve an upscale, custom furniture look that blends beautifully with the rest of the space.

◆ If your budget permits, consider automated, rotating closet racks, such as those you see at the dry cleaning store, to keep clothing organized and easily accessible.

◆ Create a soothing, restful ambiance with chandeliers set on dimmers, candles on tub surrounds, lighting over the vanity area, and other sources of soft light.

BELOW Daylight streaming in through the windows over this inviting tub is augmented by soft light from the matching sconces and graceful chandelier.

Resource Guide

The following list of manufacturers and associations is meant to be a general guide to additional industry and product-related sources. It is not intended as a listing of products and manufacturers represented by the photographs in this book.

ASSOCIATIONS

Ceramic Tiles of Italy (Italian Tile Commission)
33 E. 67th St.
New York, NY 10065
www.italytile.com
An organization that offers consumers guidance on buying Italian ceramic tile.

Decorative Plumbing & Hardware Association
7900 Wisconsin Ave., Ste. 305
Bethesda, MD 20814
Phone: 888-411-8477
www.dpha.net
A nonprofit organization that provides competitive advantages to its industry members.

The National Kitchen & Bath Association (NKBA)
687 Willow Grove St.
Hackettstown, NJ 07840
Phone: 800-THE-NKBA
www.nkba.org
A nonprofit trade association that provides education and leadership for the kitchen and bath industry.

National Lighting Bureau
8811 Colesville Rd., Ste. G106
Silver Spring, MD 20910
Phone: 301-587-9572
www.nlb.org
A nonprofit organization that helps consumers make educated decisions about their lighting choices.

MANUFACTURERS

American Standard
1 Centennial Ave.
Piscataway, NJ 08855
Phone: 732-980-3000
www.americanstandard-us.com
Manufactures bath products.

Aquatic Industries, Inc.
11880 RR 2243W
Leander, TX 78641
Phone: 512-259-2255
www.aquaticwhirlpools.com
Manufactures whirlpool and air baths.

Atlas Homewares
326 Mira Loma Ave.
Glendale, CA 91204
Phone: 818-240-3500
www.atlashomewares.com
Manufactures decorative hardware and bath ensembles.

Basco Shower Enclosures
7201 Snider Rd.
Mason, OH 45040
Phone: 800-543-1938
www.bascoshowerdoor.com
Manufactures shower enclosures.

Bristol & Bath
741 1st Ave.
King of Prussia, PA
Phone: 610-962-9329
www.bristolbath.com
Supplier of European bath products.

Broan
926 W. State St.
Hartford, WI 53027
Phone: 800-558-1711
www.broan.com
Manufactures bath ventilation products.

California Faucets
5231 Argosy Dr.
Huntington Beach, CA 92649
Phone: 800-822-8855
www.calfaucets.com
Manufactures faucets, trim, and accessories.

Caroma
Phone: 800-605-4218
www.caromausa.com
Manufactures water-conserving toilets.

Cosentino USA
13124 Trinity Dr.
Stafford, TX 77477
Phone: 281-494-7277
www.silestoneusa.com
Manufactures Silestone natural-quartz surfacing.

Crystal Cabinet Works, Inc.
1100 Crystal Dr.
Princeton, MN 55371
Phone: 763-389-4187
www.crystalcabinets.com
Manufactures bath vanities.

Danze
2500 Internationale Pkwy.
Woodridge, IL 60517
Phone: 630-679-1420
danze-online.com
Manufactures showerheads, faucets, and bath accessories.

Decolav
424 S.W. 12th Ave.
Deerfield Beach, FL 33442
Phone: 561-274-2110
www.decolav.com
Manufactures bath sinks and vanities.

Dura Supreme Cabinetry
300 Dura Dr.
Howard Lake, MN 55349
Phone: 320-543-3872
www.durasupreme.com
Manufactures bath vanities.

Fairmont Designs
6950 Noritsu Ave.
Buena Park, CA 90620
Phone: 714-670-1171
www.fairmontdesigns.com
Manufactures bath vanities.

Graff
3701 W. Burnham St.
Milwaukee, WI 53215
Phone: 800-954-4723
www.graff-faucets.com
Manufactures faucets and showers.

Jaclo Industries
129 Dermody St.
Cranford, NJ 07016
Phone: 800-852-3906
www.jaclo.com
Manufactures bath accessories and grab bars.

Jacuzzi Whirlpool Bath
14801 Quorum Dr., #550
Dallas, TX 75254
Phone: 800-288-4002
www.jacuzzi.com
Manufactures whirlpool baths, showers, toilets, and lavs.

Julien
935 Lachance St.
Quebec City, QC Canada G1P 2H3
Phone: 866-901-5624
www.julien.ca
Manufactures bath sinks, lavs, and bath suites.

Kallista
444 Highland Dr., MS 032
Kohler, WI 53044
Phone: 888-4KALLISTA
www.kallista.com
Manufactures bath suites, sinks, and faucets.

The Kohler Co.
444 Highland Dr.
Kohler, WI 53044
Phone: 800-4-KOHLER
www.kohler.com
Manufactures tubs, whirlpools, shower systems, sinks, faucets, toilets, and bath suites.

Lasco Bathware
8101 E. Kaiser Blvd., #130
Anaheim, CA 92808
Phone: 800-945-2726
www.lascobathware.com
Manufactures whirlpools, steam showers, and tubs.

Moen Inc.
25300 Al Moen Dr.
North Olmsted, OH 44070
Phone: 440-962-2000
www.moen.com
Manufactures faucets, showerheads, and sinks.

Resource Guide

Mr. Steam
43-20 34th St.
Long Island City, NY 11101
Phone: 800-76-STEAM
www.mrsteam.com
Manufactures steam bath generators, towel warmers, sauna heaters, and sauna rooms.

MTI Whirlpools
670 N. Price Rd.
Sugar Hill, GA 30518
Phone: 800-783-8827
www.mtiwhirlpools.com
Manufactures whirlpool baths, air baths, and soaking tubs.

Neptune
6835 Rue Picard
Saint-Hyacinthe, QC Canada J2S 1H3
Phone: 888-366-7058
www.neptuneb.com
Manufactures sanitaryware, tubs, toilets, and sinks.

NYLOFT Kitchens & Home Interiors
6 W. 20th St.
New York, NY 10011
Phone: 212-206-7400
www.nyloft.net
Manufactures bath vanities, mirrors, sinks, and accessories.

Omega Cabinetry
1205 Peters Dr.
Waterloo, IA 50703
Phone: 319-235-5700
www.omegacabinetry.com
Manufactures bath vanities.

Questech
92 Park St.
Rutland, VT 05701
Phone: 802-773-1228
www.questech.com
Manufactures decorative metal and stone tiles.

Rich Maid Kabinetry, LLC
633 W. Lincoln Ave.
Myerstown, PA 17067
Phone: 717-866-2112
www.richmaidkabinetry.com
Manufactures bath vanities.

Rohl LLC
3 Parker
Irvine, CA 92618
Phone: 800-777-9762
www.rohlhome.com
Manufactures luxury bath faucets, showerheads, fittings, and accessories.

Robern, Inc.
701 N. Wilson Ave.
Bristol, PA 19007
Phone: 215-826-9800
www.robern.com
Manufactures medicine cabinets.

Sea Gull Lighting/Ambiance Lighting Systems
301 W. Washington St.
Riverside, NJ 08075
Phone: 856-764-0500
www.seagulllighting.com
Manufactures lighting products.

Seura
3190 Holmgren Way Rd.
Green Bay, WI 54304
Phone: 800-957-3872
www.seura.com
Manufactures television mirrors, illuminated mirrors, and speaker systems.

St. Charles Cabinetry
215 Diller Ave.
New Holland, PA 17557
Phone: 717-351-1700
stcharlescabinetry.biz
Manufactures bath vanities.

Stone Forest
213 S. Saint Francis Dr.
Santa Fe, NM 87501
Phone: 888-682-2987
www.stoneforest.com
Manufactures stone vessels and tubs.

Thermasol
2255 Union Pl.
Simi Valley, CA 93065
Phone: 800-776-0711
www.thermasol.com
Manufactures steambaths and accessories.

THG USA
6601 Lyons Rd.
Coconut Creek, FL 33073
Phone: 954-425-8225
www.thgusa.com
Manufactures luxury faucets and accessories.

UltraGlas, Inc.
9200 Gazette Ave.
Chatsworth, CA 91311
Phone: 800-777-2332
www.ultraglas.com
Manufactures shower enclosures, flooring, lighting, and glass accessories.

Villeroy & Boch
3 S. Middlesex Ave.
Monroe Township, NJ 08831
Phone: 877-505-5350
www.villeroy-boch.com
Manufactures bath collections, whirlpool systems, and tile.

Walker Zanger
13190 Telfair Ave.
Sylmar, CA 91342
Phone: 818-256-1543
www.walkerzanger.com
Manufactures decorative tile.

Watermark Designs
491 Wortman Ave.
Spring Creek, NY 11208
Phone: 800-842-7277
www.watermark-designs.com
Manufactures bath faucets, accessories, and lighting.

Wellborn Cabinet, Inc.
38669 Hwy. 77
Ashland, AL 36251
Phone: 800-336-8040
www.wellborn.com
Manufactures bath vanities.

Westover Co.
5708 F St.
Omaha, NE 68117
Phone: 402-397-3344
Manufactures towel warmers, faucets, and shower systems.

Whirlpool Corp.
2000 M-63 North
Benton Harbor, MI 49022
Phone: 800-253-3977
www.insideadvantage.com
Manufactures kitchen appliances.

Wood-Mode, Inc.
One Second St.
Kreamer, PA 17833
Phone: 570-374-2711
www.woodmode.com
Manufactures bath vanities.

Woongjin Coway Co., Ltd.
www.coway.com
Manufactures digital bidets, and water and air filtration systems.

Yorktowne Cabinetry
P.O. Box 231, 100 Redco Ave.
Red Lion, PA 17356
Phone: 800-777-0065
www.yorktownecabinetry.com
Manufactures bath vanities.

Zehnder America, Inc.
540 Portsmouth Ave.
Greenland, NH 03840
Phone: 603-422-6700
www.zehnderamerica.com
Manufactures electric towel radiators.

Glossary

Absorption (light): The energy (wavelengths) not reflected by an object or substance. The color of a substance depends on the wavelength reflected.

Accent lighting: A type of light that highlights an area or object to emphasize that aspect of a room's character.

Accessible design: Design that accommodates persons with physical disabilities.

Accessories: Towel racks, soap dishes, and other items specifically designed for use in the bath.

Adaptable design: Design that can be easily changed to accommodate a person with disabilities.

Ambient light: General illumination that surrounds a room. There is no visible source of the light.

Anti-scald valve (pressure-balancing valve): A single-control fitting that contains a piston that automatically responds to changes in line water pressure to maintain temperature; the value blocks an abrupt drop or rise in temperature.

Apron: The front extension of a bathtub that runs from the rim to the floor.

Awning window: A window with a single framed-glass panel. It is hinged at the top to swing out when it is open.

Backlighting: Illumination coming from a source behind or at the side of an object.

Barrier-free fixtures: Fixtures specifically designed for disabled individuals who use wheelchairs or who have limited mobility.

Basin: A shallow sink.

Base cabinet: A cabinet that rests on the floor under a countertop or vanity.

Base plan: A map of an existing bathroom that shows detailed measurements and the location of fixtures and their permanent elements.

Bidet: A bowl-shaped fixture that supplies water for personal hygiene. It looks similar to a toilet.

Built-in: A cabinet, shelf, medicine chest, or other storage unit that is recessed into the wall.

Bump out: Living space created by cantilevering the floor and ceiling joists (or adding to a floor slab) and extending the exterior wall of a room.

Candlepower (Cp): The intensity of light measured at the light source.

Cantilever: A structural beam supported on one end. A cantilever can be used to support a small addition.

Casement window: A window that consists of one framed-glass panel that is hinged on the side. It swings outward from the opening at the turn of a crank.

Centerline: The dissecting line through the center of an object, such as a sink.

CFM: An abbreviation that refers to the amount of cubic feet of air that is moved per minute by an exhaust fan.

Clearance: The amount of space between two fixtures, the centerlines of two fixtures, or a fixture and an obstacle, such as a wall. Clearances may be mandated by building codes.

Code: A locally or nationally enforced mandate regarding structural design, materials, plumbing, or electrical systems that states what you can or cannot do when you build or remodel. Codes are intended to protect standards of health, safety, and land use.

Color rendition index (CRI): Measures the way a light source renders color. The higher the index number, the closer colors illuminated by the light source resemble how they appear in sunlight.

Contemporary style: A style of decoration or architecture that is modern and pertains to what is current.

Combing: A painting technique that involves using a small device with teeth or grooves over a wet painted surface to create a grained effect.

Correlated color temperature (CCT): A value assigned to a fluorescent lamp indicating the warmth or coolness of the light it produces.

Dimmer Switch: A switch that can vary the intensity of the light source that it controls.

Downlighting: A lighting technique that illuminates objects or areas from above.

Double-hung window: A window that consists of two framed-glass panels that slide open vertically, guided by a metal or wood track.

Duct: A tube or passage for venting indoor air to the outside.

Enclosure: Any material used to form a shower or tub stall, such as glass, glass block, or a tile wall.

Faux painting: Various painting techniques that mimic wood, marble, and other stones.

Fittings: The plumbing devices that transport water to the fixtures. These can include showerheads, faucets, and spouts. Also pertains to hardware and some accessories, such as towel racks, soap dishes, and toilet-paper dispensers.

Fixture spacing: The amount of space included between ambient light fixtures to achieve an even field of illumination in a given area.

Fixed window: A window that cannot be opened. It is usually a decorative unit, such as a half-round or Palladian-style window.

Fixture: Any fixed part of the structural design, such as tubs, bidets, toilets, and lavatories.

Fluorescent lamp: An energy-efficient light source made of a tube with an interior phosphorus coating that glows when energized by electricity.

Foot-candle (Fc): A unit that is used to measure the brightness produced by a lamp. A foot-candle is equal to one lumen per square foot of surface.

Form: The shape and structure of space or an object.

Full bath: A bath that includes a toilet, lavatory, and bathing fixtures, such as a tub or shower.

Glass blocks: Decorative building blocks made of translucent glass used for non-load-bearing walls to allow passage of light.

Glazing (walls): A technique for applying a thinned, tinted wash of translucent color to a dry undercoat of paint.

Ground-fault circuit interrupter (GFCI): A safety circuit breaker that compares the amount of current entering a receptacle with the amount leaving. If there is a discrepancy of 0.005 volt, the GFCI breaks the circuit in a fraction of a second. GFCIs are required by the National Electrical Code in areas that are subject to dampness.

Grout: A binder and filler applied in the joints between ceramic tile.

Glossary

Halogen bulb: A bulb filled with halogen gas, a substance that causes the particles of tungsten to be redeposited onto the tungsten filament. This process extends the lamp's life and makes the light whiter and brighter.

Half bath (powder room): A bathroom that contains only a toilet and a sink.

Highlight: The lightest tone in a room.

Incandescent lamp: A bulb that contains a conductive filament through which current flows. The current reacts with an inert gas inside the bulb, which makes the filament glow.

Intensity: Strength of a color.

Jets: Nozzles installed behind the walls of tubs or showers that pump out pressurized streams of water.

Joist: Set in a parallel fashion, these framing members support the boards of a ceiling or a floor.

Lavatory or lav: A fixed bowl or basin with running water and a drainpipe that is used for washing.

Load-bearing wall: A wall that supports a structure's vertical load. Openings in any load-bearing wall must be reinforced to carry the live and dead weight of the structure's load.

Lumen: A term that refers to the intensity of light measured at a light source that is used for general or ambient lighting.

Muntins: Framing members of a window that divide the panes of glass.

Palette: A range of colors that complement each other.

Pedestal: A stand-alone lavatory with a basin and supporting column in one piece.

Pocket door: A door that opens by sliding inside the wall, as opposed to a conventional door that opens into a room.

Pressure-balancing valve: Also known as a surge protector or anti-scald device. It is a control that prevents surges of hot or cold water in faucets by equalizing the amounts of hot and cold water pumped out at any time.

Proportion: The relationship of one object to another.

Radiant floor heat: A type of heating brought into a room via electrical wire or pipes (to carry hot water) that have been installed under the floor. As the pipes or electrical wire heats up, the flooring material warms and heat rises into the room.

Ragging: A painting technique that uses a crumbled piece of cloth to apply or remove small amounts of wet paint to create a pattern or texture.

Reflectance levels: The amount of light that is reflected from a colored surface, such as a tile wall or painted surface.

Roof window: A horizontal window that is installed on the roof. Roof windows are ventilating.

Scale: The size of a room or object.

Schematic: A detailed diagram of systems within a home.

Sconce: A decorative wall bracket, sometimes made of iron or glass, that shields a bulb.

Skylight: A framed opening in the roof that admits sunlight into the house. It can be covered with either a flat glass panel or a plastic dome.

Sight line: The natural line of sight the eye travels when looking into or around a room.

Sliding window: Similar to a double-hung window turned on its side. The glass panels slide horizontally.

Snap-in grilles: Ready-made rectangular and diamond-pattern grilles that snap into a window sash and create the look of a true divided-light window.

Soffit: A boxed-in area just below the ceiling and above the upper cabinets.

Space reconfiguration: A design term that is used to describe the reallocation of interior space without adding on.

Sponging: A paint technique that uses a small sponge to apply or remove small amounts of wet paint to create a pattern or texture on a surface.

Spout: The tube or pipe from which water gushes out of a faucet.

Stencil: A design cut out of plastic or cardboard. When paint is applied to the cutout area, the design will be reproduced on a surface.

Stud: The vertical member of a framed wall, usually placed every 16 inches on center. A stud provides structural framing and is usually covered with drywall or plywood.

Subfloor: The flooring applied directly to the floor joists on top of which the finished floor rests.

Surround: The enclosure and area around a tub or shower. A surround may include steps and a platform, as well as the tub itself.

Task lighting: Lighting designed to illuminate a particular task, such as shaving.

Tone: The degree of lightness or darkness of a color.

Traditional style: A style of decoration or architecture (typically of the eighteenth and nineteenth centuries) that employs forms that have been repeated for generations without major changes.

Trompe l'oeil: French for "fool the eye." A paint technique that creates a photographically real illusion of space or objects.

True divided-light window: A window composed of multiple glass panes that are divided by and held together by muntins.

Universal design: Products and designs that are easy to use by people of all ages, heights, and varying physical abilities.

Vanity: The countertop and cabinet unit that supports a sink. The vanity is usually included in the bathroom for storage purposes. It may also be used as a dressing table.

Whirlpool: A special tub that includes motorized jets behind the walls of the tub for water massages.

Index

Index

Photo and Designer Credits

Page 1: design: Karen Dry, Garrett Interiors **page 2:** Peter Krupenye, architect: Carol Kurth, AIA, The Office of Carol J.W. Kurth, AIA Architect **page 6:** courtesy of Aquatic Industries, Inc. **page 8:** courtesy of Villeroy & Boch **page 9:** design: Gary White, CMKBD, CID, Kitchen & Bath Design **page 10:** design: Sawhill Custom Kitchens & Design, Inc. and Plato Woodwork, Inc.**page 11:** Seura **page 12:** Courtesy of Kohler Co. **page 14:** *top* courtesy of Moen Inc.; *bottom* courtesy of Kohler Co. **page 15:** design: Peter Salerno, Peter Salerno Inc. **page 16:** *left* Rohl LLC; *right* Tim Buchman, architect: Dennis E. Yates, AIA **page 18:** *top* courtesy of Danze; *bottom* courtesy of Bristol & Bath **page 19:** courtesy of MTI Whirlpools **page 21:** courtesy of Questech **pages 22–23:** *both* courtesy of Kohler Co. **page 24:** *top* design: Bev Adams, CMKBD, Interior Intuitions, Inc.; *bottom* courtesy of Kohler Co. **page 25:** courtesy of Moen Inc. **pages 26–30:** Peter Krupenye, architect: Carol Kurth, AIA, The Office of Carol J.W. Kurth, AIA Architect **page 32:** design: Karen Dry, Garrett Interiors **page 33:** *top* design: Karen Dry, Garrett Interiors; *bottom* Peter Krupenye, architect: Carol Kurth, AIA, The Office of Carol J.W. Kurth, AIA Architect **page 34:** Cheryl Hamilton-Gray, Hamilton-Gray Design, Inc. **page 35:** *top* design: Cheryl Hamilton-Gray, Hamilton-Gray Design, Inc.; *bottom* design: Julie Stoner, ASID, CKD, Kitchen & Bath Galleria **page 36:** Peter Krupenye, architect: Carol Kurth, AIA, The Office of Carol J.W. Kurth, AIA Architect **page 38:** *top* Peter Krupenye, architect: Carol Kurth, AIA, The Office of Carol J.W. Kurth, AIA Architect; *bottom* design: Cheryl Hamilton-Gray, Hamilton-Gray Design, Inc. **page 39:** Peter Krupenye, architect: Carol Kurth, AIA, The Office of Carol J.W. Kurth, AIA Architect **page 40:** courtesy of JSG Oceana **page 41:** Peter Krupenye, architect: Carol Kurth, AIA, The Office of Carol J.W. Kurth, AIA Architect **page 42:** design: Karen Dry, Garrett Interiors **pages 43–44:** *both* Peter Krupenye, architect: Carol Kurth, AIA, The Office of Carol J.W. Kurth, AIA Architect **page 45:** *top left &* *bottom* design: Cheryl Hamilton-Gray, Hamilton-Gray Design, Inc.; *top right* courtesy St. Charles Cabinetry; *bottom* Cheryl Hamilton-Gray, Hamilton-Gray Design, Inc. **page 47:** courtesy of Moen Inc. **page 48:** design: Patricia Davis Brown, Patricia Davis Brown Fine Cabinetry, Inc. **page 50:** courtesy of UltraGlas, Inc. **page 51:** Peter Krupenye, architect: Carol Kurth, AIA, The Office of Carol J.W. Kurth, AIA Architect **page 52:** courtesy of Kohler Co. **page 53:** *top* courtesy of Kohler Co.; *bottom* courtesy of MTI Whirlpools **page 54:** *left* courtesy of Rohl LLC; *right* design: Julie Stoner, ASID, CKD, Kitchen & Bath Galleria **page 55:** courtesy of Jaclo Industries **page 56:** design: Karen Dry, Garrett Interiors **page 57:** courtesy of Basco Shower Enclosures **page 58–59:** *both* courtesy of Kohler Co. **page 60:** courtesy of St. Charles Cabinetry **page 62:** courtesy of Villeroy & Boch **page 63:** *top* courtesy of Aquatic Industries, Inc.; *bottom* Peter Krupenye, architect: Carol Kurth, AIA, The Office of Carol J.W. Kurth, AIA Architect **page 64:** courtesy of Westover Co. **page 65:** *top* courtesy of Kohler Co.; *bottom* courtesy of Lasco Bathware **page 66:** courtesy of Julien **page 67:** *top* courtesy of Jacuzzi Whirlpool Bath; *bottom* courtesy of Neptune **pages 68–70:** *both* courtesy of NYLOFT Kitchens & Home Interiors **page 71:** design: Sawhill Custom Kitchens & Design, Inc. **page 72:** design: Fairmont Designs **page 73:** *top* design: Sawhill Custom Kitchens & Design, Inc. and Plato Woodwork, Inc.; *bottom* courtesy of Dura Supreme Cabinetry **page 74:** courtesy of NYLOFT Kitchens & Home Interiors **page 75:** *top* courtesy of Rich Maid Kabinetry, LLC; *bottom* courtesy of NYLOFT Kitchens & Home Interiors **page 76:** *left* courtesy of Omega Cabinetry; *right* design: Artistic Tile **page 77:** courtesy of Yorktowne Cabinetry **pages 78–79:** *left* design: Drury Design; *right* courtesy of Omega Cabinetry **page 80:** courtesy of Omega Cabinetry **page 81:** design: Sawhill Custom Kitchens & Design, Inc. & Paragon Home Fashions **page 82:** *top* design: Patricia Davis Brown, Patricia Davis Brown Fine Cabinetry, Inc.; *bottom* Peter Krupenye, architect: Carol Kurth, AIA, The Office of Carol J.W. Kurth, AIA Architect **page 83:** courtesy of Binns Kitchen & Bath Design, design: Anthony Binns, Beverly Binns and Tony Hunt **page 84:** design: Sawhill Custom Kitchens & Design, Inc. **page 85:** courtesy of Wellborn Cabinet, Inc. **page 86:** courtesy of Walker Zanger **page 89:** *top right & left* design: Artistic Tile; *bottom* courtesy of Walker Zanger **page 90:** courtesy of Villeroy & Boch **page 91:** *top* courtesy of Stone Impressions; *bottom* courtesy of Questech **page 92:** design: Artistic Tile **page 93:** *top* Maxwell MacKenzie, design: courtesy of Italian Trade Commission; *bottom left* courtesy of Binns Kitchen & Bath Design, design: Tony Hunt; *bottom right* courtesy of Cosentino USA/Silestone **page 94:** *top* design: Cheryl Hamilton-Gray, Hamilton-Gray Design, Inc.; *bottom* courtesy of Consentino USA/Silestone **page 95:** courtesy of Walker Zanger **page 96:** courtesy of Consentino USA/Silestone **page 97:** courtesy of Binns Kitchen & Bath Design, design: Anthony Binns, Beverly Binns and Tony Hunt **page 98:** design: Artistic Tile **page 99:** courtesy of Walker Zanger **page 100:** *top left* courtesy of Walker Zanger; *top right & bottom* courtesy of Italian Trade Commission **pages 101–104:** *all* design: Artistic Tile **pages 105–106:** *both* courtesy of Italian Trade Commission **page 108:** courtesy of Kohler Co. **page 109:** courtesy of Decolav **page 110:** courtesy of Kohler Co. **page 111:** courtesy of Moen Inc. **page 112:** *top right & left* courtesy of Kohler Co.; *bottom* courtesy of Delta Faucet **page 113:** design: Drury Design **page 114:** *left* courtesy of Delta Faucet; *right* courtesy of Moen Inc. **page 115:** courtesy of Delta Faucet **page 116:** *left* courtesy of Moen Inc.; *right* courtesy of California Faucets **page 117:** *top* courtesy of California Faucets; *bottom* courtesy of Kallista **page 118:** Mike Kaskel of Kaskel Architectural Photography, design: Mark T. White, Kitchen Encounters **page 121:** *top* courtesy of Kohler Co.; *bottom* courtesy of Moen Inc. **page 122:** design: Drury Design **page 123:** *top left* courtesy of Kohler Co.; *right* courtesy of California Faucets; *bottom left* courtesy of THG USA **pages 124–126:** *both* design: Drury Design **page 127:**

Maxwell MacKenzie, courtesy of Italian Trade Commission **page 128:** Gary White, CMKBD, CID, Kitchen & Bath Design **page 129:** courtesy of Sea Gull Lighting/Ambiance Lighting Systems **page 130–132:** *all* design: Drury Design **page 133:** *top* John Nasta Photography, design: Jennifer B. Pippin, Pippin Home Designs, Inc.; *bottom* Michael Gullon of Phoenix Photographic, design: Mark T. White, Kitchen Encounters **page 134:** courtesy of Sea Gull Lighting/Ambiance Lighting Systems **pages 135–136:** courtesy of Omega Cabinetry **page 137:** *top right* courtesy of Villeroy & Boch; *left* courtesy of Sea Gull Lighting/Ambiance Lighting Systems; *bottom left* courtesy of Omega Cabinetry **page 138:** courtesy of Kohler Co. **page 139:** *top* courtesy of MTI Whirlpools; *bottom* courtesy of Sea Gull Lighting/Ambiance Lighting Systems **page 140:** *bottom left* design: Artistic Tile; *top right* courtesy of Binns Kitchen & Bath Design, design: Anthony Binns, Beverly Binns and Tony Hunt **page 141:** design: Drury Design **page 142–143:** *both* courtesy of Sea

Gull Lighting/Ambiance Lighting Systems **pages 144–147:** *all* courtesy of Kohler Co. **page 148:** courtesy of Jacuzzi Whirlpool Bath **page 149:** *top* courtesy of Thermasol; *center* courtesy of Mr.Steam **pages 150–157:** *all* courtesy of Kohler Co. **page 159:** courtesy of Seura **page 160:** courtesy of Kohler Co. **page 162:** *top* courtesy of Watermark Designs; *bottom* courtesy of Kohler Co. **page 163:** Sawhill Custom Kitchens & Design, Inc. **page 164:** courtesy of Stone Forest **page 165:** *bottom left* courtesy of Kohler Co.; *top right* Alex Anton, design: Candice Adler, Candice Adler Design **page 166:** *top* courtesy of Kohler Co.; *bottom* courtesy of THG USA **page 167:** courtesy of Zehnder America, Inc. **page 168:** *top right* courtesy of Atlas Homewares; *left* courtesy of THG USA **page 169:** courtesy of Robern, Inc. **page 170:** *top left* Alex Anton, design: Candice Adler, Candice Adler Design; *bottom* courtesy of Jaclo Industries **page 171:** courtesy of Creative Specialties International **page 173:** courtesy of Kohler Co., A Shell

Collector's Bath by Harry Heissmann **page 174:** design: Diane Plesset, ASID, CMKBD, DP Design **page 176:** design: Jim Dase, Abruzzo Kitchens **page 177:** courtesy of Kohler Co. **page 178:** Treve Johnson Photography, design: Mollyanne Sherman, CKD, CBD, CID, MAC Design **pages 180–181:** *both* courtesy of Kohler Co. **page 182:** courtesy of Kohler Co., Woodland Sanctuary by Nikki Blustin and Oliver Heath **page 183:** courtesy of Kohler Co., Cabochon Room by Jamie Drake **pages 184–185:** courtesy of Kohler Co. **pages 186–187:** *all* courtesy of Wellborn Cabinet, Inc. **page 188:** courtesy of Wood-Mode, Inc. **page 189:** *top left* courtesy of Wellborn Cabinet, Inc.; *top middle, top right, bottom* courtesy of Wood-Mode, Inc. **page 190:** courtesy of KitchenAid **page 193:** design: Drury Design **page 200:** courtesy of Binns Kitchen & Bath Design, design: Anthony Binns, Beverly Binns and Tony Hunt **page 205:** Jim Mims, design: Lori Jo Krengel, CMKBD, Kitchens by Krengel, Inc. **pages 207:** courtesy of Kohler Co.

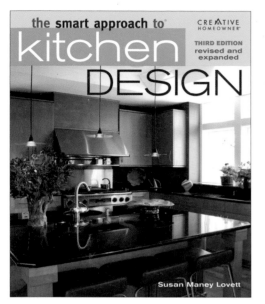

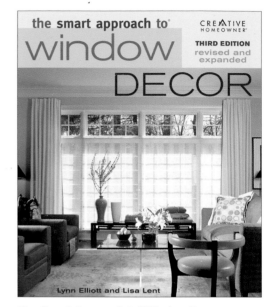
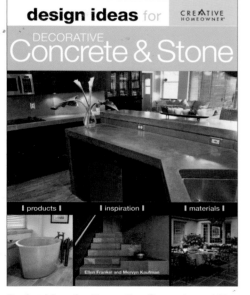
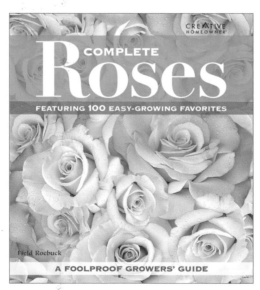
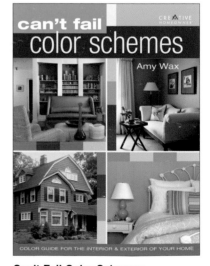